1969 AMVETS 25th Anniversary

1970 NEC meets in Berlin/Seeks support for POW effort

1971 First thrift store opens on Georgia Ave. in Washington, D.C.

1972 Auxiliary hosts Women's Forum on National Security

1973 *The National AMVET* resumes monthly publication as tabloid

1974 Auxiliary adopts John Tracy Clinic as national program

1975 Vietnam era ends/Amnesty-for-draft evaders legislation defeated

1976 First Auxiliary Humanitarian Award presented to Rep. Corrine C. Boggs

1977 Stand taken in support of Senate Veterans' Affairs Committee

1978 New carillon dedicated at Arlington Cemetery

1979 Ground broken for new headquarters on Forbes Blvd. in Lanham, Md.

1980 Appeals made to elevate VA/Third headquarters dedicated

1981 Gramm-Latta Amendment endorsed

1982 Because We Care Day instituted/Vietnam Veterans Memorial dedicated

1983 Assistance provided families of marines wounded in Lebanon

1984 New memorial wall dedicated/Active military accepted as members

1985 AMVETS National Memorial Carillon dedicated

1986 Statue of Liberty restored/AMVETS contributes $100,000 to project

1987 First Independent Budget produced

1988 VA achieves cabinet-level status as Department of Veterans Affairs

1989 AMVETS Against Drug and Alcohol Abuse Program started

1990 National guardsmen and reservists accepted as members

1991 *Arizona* Memorial Room dedicated/Gulf War ends

1992 Massive veterans' protest stops VA rural health care initiative

1993 AMVETS-Toyota Safe Driving Challenge launched

1994 AMVETS 50th anniversary

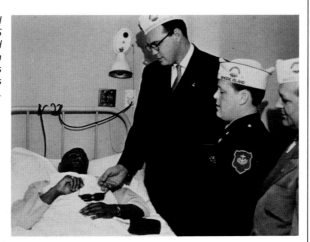

National Commander Marshall Miller and fellow AMVETS comfort a hospitalized veteran in 1952—a tradition of service that continues today in VA medical centers across the country.

AMVETS

50 YEARS OF PROUD SERVICE
TO AMERICA'S VETERANS

Founders

Lamarr Bailey
William E. Blake
George E. Burke
Thomas H. Chunn
Floyd Cooper, Jr.
Carl G.Freudenberg
Albert C. Geremia
Glen A. Harmon
Horacio C. Holdridge
Roy E. Hughes
Elmo W. Keel
E. Henry Miller
Paul Moody
Claude C. Morgan
Joseph Motta
Raymond O'Brien
Edward P. Trudell
Floyd L. Williams

National Commanders

A. Leo Anderson
Berge Avadanian
Harold T. Berc
Vaughn L. Brown, Sr.
Essley B. Burdine
Winston E. Burdine
Anthony J. Caserta
Edgar C. Corry, Jr.
Warren W. Eagles, Sr.
Joseph V. Ferrino
Edwin P. Fifielski
Robert B. Gomulinski
Edmund M. Gulewicz
Ralph E. Hall
Jack W. Hardy
Donald M. Hearon
Harold A. Keats
Elmo W. Keel
James J. Kenney
James B. King
Joseph R. Koralewski
Ted Leszkiewicz
John S. Lorec
Henry J. Mahady
Robert Martin
Thomas J. McDonough
Robert A. Medairos
Marshall E. Miller
Rudolph G. Pesata
Joseph T. Piening
Ernest F. Pitochelli

Joe F. Ramsey, Jr.
Frank D. Ruggiero
Donald R. Russell
Harold S. Russell
Joseph R. Sanson
Stuart J. Satullo
Ray Sawyer
Robert W. Showalter
James L. Singler
Jimmy T. Smith
John L. Smith
Dante E. Spagnolo
Dominick L. Strada
Lincoln S. Tamraz
Paul C. Welsh
Robert L. Wilbraham
Rufus H. Wilson

National Presidents

Jane Ashley
Pearl V. Barnett
Mary S. Barrow
Jean Baxter
Ellen Bogatay
Mae Boone
Anne Brown
Dorothy R. Bull
Doris L. Burdine
Gloria I. Clark
Nita I. Cornell
Jewel W. Fifielski
Evelyn M. Flasco
Adeline P. Fogg
Toni Gomulinski
Darline Gordon
Anne E. Hall
Kathleen Hengely
Barbara S. Hinsley
Agnes P. Kolano
Evelyn Lauritson
Betty S. Lawson
Betty J. Leisure
Dorothy M. LeRoy
Sylvia Lipowski
Lila B. Longworth
Edith G. Males
June L. Miller
Marie Miller
Leah Monasterio
Ruth K. Nickerson
Alice Oana
Grace G. Osborn
Rita Potvin
Marie Redden
Margaret Rummel
Dorothy J. Bussard Ruph
Beatrice F. Russell
Lucia C. Russo
Doris G. Shrake
Ruth Singler
Kathryn N. Snyder
Aldean M. Sorrells
Dorothy J. Stoddard
Florence Stripe

Dorothy Sullivan
Betty Torner
Betty M. Wineland

Sons of AMVETS
National Commanders

James R. Brown
George W. Burral, Jr.
Daniel P. Connolly
John V. Creech
Roger Damron
Charles Kyser
Stanley L. Mellot
Richard S. Mooney, Jr.
Allan McKinney
Stephen M. Turner

Junior AMVETS
National Presidents

Judy Newlun Anske
Mark Bartell
Brian Beedon
Danalee Boysel
Jayelee Boysel
Marcia Buttelworth
David R. Cain
Kenneth T. Cain
Brian Curie
Sharon Engler
Debbie Gomulinski
Guy Hawkins
Michelle Henson
Evan Hilliard
Eugene K. Johnson
Tom Kyewski
Tim Lewis
Therese LeRoy
Ellen Mandell
Jason Mercado
Jacquelin M. Perez
Robert Runnels
Donald Savage, Jr.
Regina Schumucki
Tonya Schmuckie
Marlene South

National Sadders

Bert Blok
George Box
Henry Boyd
Ray Daniel
George Demchak
Mike Dougherty
Gerald Ewing
Edward Fabert
James Farris
Amy Mae Feluk
James J. Gattler
Al Gerhardt
Arthur Goguen
Placide Goguen
D.E. Grahame
Ken Grossman
Edward J. Haba

Danny Hart
Earl Henson
Charles F. Hill
David D. Hogan, Jr.
Thomas Jones
William Kipp
Harold Koch
Thad Males
Eva Manchester
Jasper McCain
Walter Meister
Gerald O'Callaghan
Jim Schuman
Steve Sernetko
James L. Singler
John Stegman
Hairl Thacker
Gerri Thomas
Harry Travis
John Trinidad
Peter P. Triolo
James L. Verber
Orland Wackerie
Paul C. Welsh
Paul Westbrook
Bill White

National Snappiests

Este Lee Beadles
Barbara Behymer
Virginia Bowler
Alice R.J. Bushman
Geneva E. Buzzetta
Catherine Carroll
Barbara Cech
Gloria I. Clark
Tina Cordeiro
Eileen Dixon
Nora Duclos
Jean French
Kay Gibbons
Susie Goguen
Bernadine Hammond
Charlene Hiland
Hazel Hogan
Mary Koch
Dorothy LeRoy
Mary Matthews
Henrietta McClosky
Ann Miller
Ethel M. Miller
Irene Mims
Grace G. Osborn
Pansey Preston
Shelby L. Rhodes
June Ruddell
Wileane Sperry
Helen Theorde
Evelyn Thomas
Margaret Thompson
Nora Thompson
Midren C. Townes
Betty Jane Welsh
Olga Wesloh

AMVETS

50 YEARS OF PROUD SERVICE TO AMERICA'S VETERANS

AMVETS NATIONAL HEADQUARTERS • LANHAM, MARYLAND

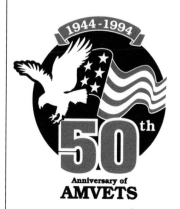

1993-94 Officers

AMVETS

National Commander
Donald M. Hearon
Vice Commanders
Arthur W. Klingel, Jr. *(membership)*
Kenneth Wolford *(programs)*
National Finance Officer
John Ricottilli, Jr.
National Judge Advocate
Marshall E. Miller
National Provost Marshal
Albert E. Woodard
National Chaplain
Rev. Francis J. Crowley
National District Commanders
James E. Blake *(I)*, Robert J. Klausing *(II)*
James A. Conner *(III)*, Charles L. Taylor *(IV)*
James W. Miller *(V)*, Harry Stephens *(VI)*

National Service Foundation

President
Robert L. Wilbraham
Vice President
Ernest F. Pitochelli, Sr.
Treasurer
John Ricottilli, Jr.
National Commander
Donald M. Hearon
National Judge Advocate
Marshall E. Miller
Trustees
James L. Singler
Joseph T. Piening
Joseph T. Kolano
Legal Counsel
Julius R. Pollatschek

Auxiliary

President
Barbara S. Hinsley
Vice Presidents
Janet St. Michel
Cathy Fishero
Brenda Kilgore
Treasurer
Janice Cloutier
Chaplain
Janice Hapner
Hospital Chairman
Linda Johnston
Parliamentarian
Doris Burdine
Americanism Officer
Virginia Sorrels
Scholarship Officer
Denice LaBatt

Sergeant-At-Arms
Louise Thacker
VAVS Representative
Marilyn Murphy
Editor/*Auxiliary News*
Carol A. King
Junior AMVETS Coordinator
Gertrude Melcher
Honors and Awards
Mary Barrow
Liaison/Legislative Officer
Betty S. Lawson

Sons of AMVETS

Commander
Charles Kyser
Vice Commanders
Stephen M. Turner *(membership)*
Brian Price *(programs)*
Finance Officer
Ed Moore
Judge Advocate
Randy Greene
Provost Marshal
Mike Kollar
Chaplain
Jason Beckler
Historian/Public Relations Officer
William Timmerman
Scholarship Chairman
Michael T. Barr
National VAVS Representative
Earl Johnston

Junior AMVETS

President
Celina Spurgeon
Senior Vice President
Patrick Schmuckie
Junior Vice President
Kelly Sue Fishero
Treasurer
Peter Cloutier
Chaplain
Chris Lawson
Public Relations Officer
Justin Culbreth
Sergeant-At-Arms
Brad Boysel
Parliamentarian
Kim Aultman

Sad Sacks

National Saddest
David E. Fishero
National Almost
(vacant)

lmost Not Quite
rthur Griffith
ational Squire
obert Brehmer
ational Hoosegow
obert Pace
ational Worm
onald Powers
ational Cut-Up
ichael A. Lizzano, Sr.
ational Noseyest
.E. Guthrie
ational Wailer
obert Middleton
ational Solemnest
homas Barr
xtra Bags
len L. Speciale
hn L. Martz, Sr.
sse D. Way
nthony Lolli
onald Webb
ichard Frame
dder #45
obert Reardon

ackettes

appiest
hyllis L. Walsh
appier
arlee Morrison
cribbling
atherine Ditman
vingest
onstance Kirk
erious
el Solak
ubbornest
ouise Thacker
licitress
elby Rhodes
crappiest
dna Wolford
ustler
elia A. Shafer
cholarship
ay Gibbons
eezer Squeezer
aire Lemoine

Staff

National
Headquarters
ational Executive Director
mes J. Kenney
ontroller
obert W. Thompson

National Directors
Michael F. Brinck *(legislative)*
Richard W. Flanagan *(public relations)*
Gregory V. Floberg *(marketing/programs)*
Noel C. Woosley *(service)*
National Assistant Directors
Veronica K. A'zera *(programs)*
Frank J. Olszewski, Jr. *(membership)*
National Quartermaster
Stephanie K. Ellis
National Printer
Elias S. Lambrakopoulos
Assistants
Nanette E. Dobson *(executive)*
Earnest E. Howell *(legislative)*
Debbie B. Sanford *(controller)*
Tonya L. Swann *(public relations)*
Michele A. Towle *(administrative)*
Specialists
Barbara A. Dupont, *(insurance/personnel)*
Rita J. McGuigan *(program)*
Stephen G. Single *(computer)*
Executive Meeting Planner
Meg Slentz-Nagy
Maintenance Supervisor
Robert D. Terwilliger
Executive Secretaries
Kathryn D. Wisilosky *(service)*
Carolyn M. Woosley *(membership)*
Programs Secretary
Sharon E. Cox
Membership Data Technician
Remonia Chaplin
Data Entry Clerk
Kameko K. Plater
National Receptionist/
Switchboard Operator
Lea K. Cole

National Service
Foundation
Executive Director
Joe F. Ramsey, Jr.
Assistant Executive Director
Frank T. Huray
Comptroller
Robert W. Thompson
Director of Planned Giving
John S. Peppers
Managers
Michael H. Charters *(laser operations)*
Robert S. Gujral *(production/direct mail)*
Assistant to Comptroller
Christel A. Gray
Accounting Assistants
E. Diane Simons
Vera Nebesky
Junior Accountant
Kathleen Douglas
Analysts
Mary Lou Callahan *(cost)*
Stephen G. Single *(computer)*

Executive Secretary
Sandra G. McDonald
Secretary to Comptroller
Jill A. Devaney
Sales/Laser Operations
Karen A. Cordone
Laser Operations
Richard D. Karstetter
Postal Operations
John R. Harvey
Supervisor/Mail Room
Beverly F. Lewis
Cashiers/Mail Room
Colleen S. Mercer
Bettye J. Brown
Annette L. Lindsay
Receptionist
Rose Mary T. Checho

Auxiliary
Administrative Assistant
Kathleen S. Culbreth
Office Manager
Marjorie C. Mattocks

Sons of AMVETS
Coordinator
Gilbert Garza
Executive Secretary
Sarah Myer

Junior AMVETS
AMVETS Coordinator
Raymond Cloutier
Auxiliary Coordinator
Gertrude Melcher

Sad Sacks
Executive Secretary
Catherine Ditman

Sackettes
Administrative Director
Norman C. Bradford

AMVETS National Headquarters
4647 Forbes Boulevard
Lanham, MD 20706-4380

©AMVETS (American Veterans of
World War II, Korea and Vietnam)
All Rights Reserved. Published 1994
Printed in the United States of America

Library of Congress
Catalog Card Number: 94-72575

ISBN 0-9642526-0-0

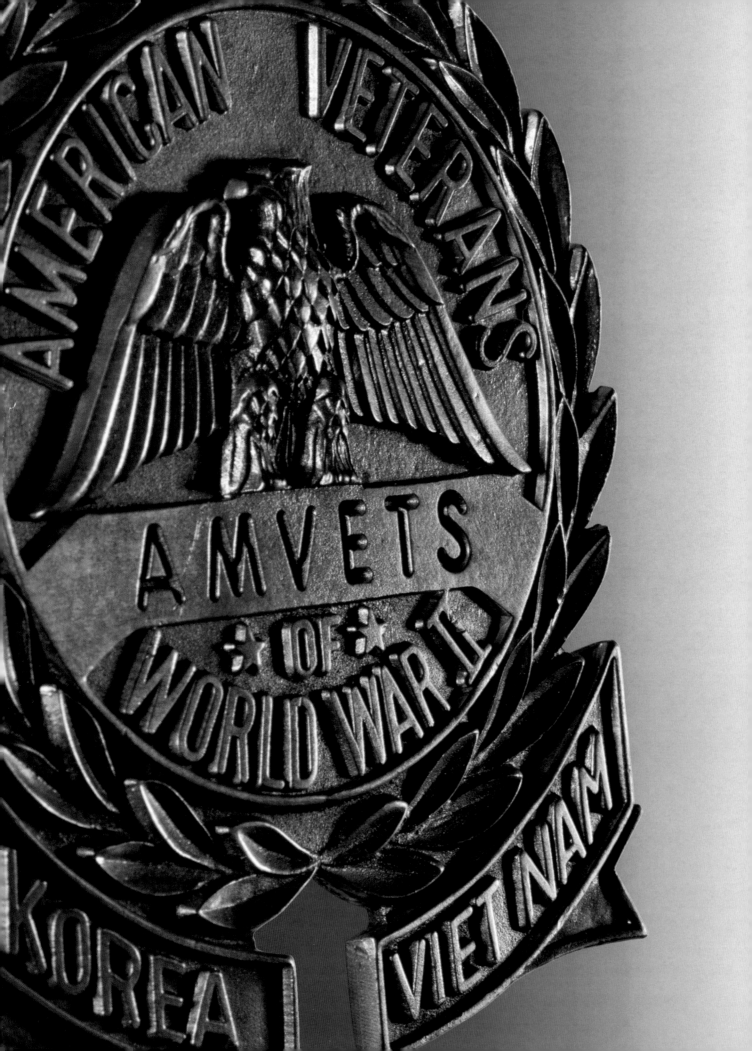

Contents

Editor/Designer
Richard W. Flanagan

Associate Editor
Tonya L. Swann

Editorial Assistant
LaSandra M. Purnell

Production
Graphica
Lanham, Md.

Printing
Stephenson
Alexandria, Va.

Honolulu Star-Bulletin 1ST EXTRA

Evening Bulletin, Est. 1882, No. 11779
Hawaiian Star, Vol. XLVIII, No. 15338
8 PAGES—HONOLULU, TERRITORY OF HAWAII, U. S. A., SUNDAY, DECEMBER 7, 1941—8 PAGES
★ PRICE FIVE CENTS

WAR!

(Associated Press by Transpacific Telephone)

SAN FRANCISCO, Dec. 7.—President Roosevelt announced this morning that Japanese planes had attacked Manila and Pearl Harbor.

OAHU BOMBED BY JAPANESE PLANES

SIX KNOWN DEAD, 21 INJURED, AT EMERGENCY HOSPITAL

Attack Made On Island's Defense Areas

By UNITED PRESS

WASHINGTON, Dec. 7. —Text of a White House announcement detailing the attack on the Hawaiian islands is:

"The Japanese attacked Pearl Harbor from the air and all naval and military activities on the island of Oahu, principal American base in the Hawaiian islands."

Oahu was attacked at 7:55 this morning by Japanese planes.

The Rising Sun, emblem of Japan, was seen on plane wing tips.

Wave after wave of bombers streamed through the clouded morning sky from the southwest and flung their missiles on a city resting in peaceful Sabbath calm.

According to an unconfirmed report received at the governor's office, the Japanese force that attacked Oahu reached island waters aboard two small airplane carriers.

It was also reported that at the governor's office either an attempt had been made to bomb the USS Lexington, or that it had been bombed.

CITY IN UPROAR

Within 10 minutes the city was in an uproar. As bombs fell in many parts of the city, and in defense areas the defenders of the islands went into quick action.

Army intelligence officers at Ft. Shafter announced officially shortly after 9 a. m. the fact of the bombardment by an enemy but long previous army and navy had taken immediate measures in defense.

"Oahu is under a sporadic air raid," the announcement said.

"Civilians are ordered to stay off the streets until further notice."

CIVILIANS ORDERED OFF STREETS

The army has ordered that all civilians stay off the streets and highways and not use telephones.

Evidence that the Japanese attack has registered some hits was shown by three billowing pillars of smoke in the Pearl Harbor and Hickam field area.

All navy personnel and civilian defense workers, with the exception of women, have been ordered to duty at Pearl Harbor.

The Pearl Harbor highway was immediately a mass of racing cars.

A trickling stream of injured people began pouring into the city emergency hospital a few minutes after the bombardment started.

Thousands of telephone calls almost swamped the Mutual Telephone Co., which put extra operators on duty.

At The Star-Bulletin office the phone calls deluged the single operator and it was impossible for this newspaper, for sometime, to handle the flood of calls. Here also an emergency operator was called.

HOUR OF ATTACK—7:55 A. M.

An official army report from department headquarters, made public shortly before 11, is that the first attack was at 7:55 a. m.

Witnesses said they saw at least 50 airplanes over Pearl Harbor.

The attack centered in the Pearl Harbor, Army authorities said:

"The rising sun was seen on the wing tips of the airplanes."

Although martial law has not been declared officially, the city of Honolulu was operating under M-Day conditions.

It is reliably reported that enemy objectives under attack were Wheeler field Hickam field, Kaneohe bay and naval air station and Pearl Harbor.

Some enemy planes were reported shot down.

The body of the pilot was seen in a plane burning at Wahiawa.

Oahu appeared to be taking calmly after the first uproar of queries.

ANTIAIRCRAFT GUNS IN ACTION

First indication of the raid came shortly before 8 this morning when antiaircraft guns around Pearl Habor began sending up a thunderous barrage.

At the same time a vast cloud of black smoke arose from the naval base and also from Hickam field where flames could be seen.

BOMB NEAR GOVERNOR'S MANSION

Shortly before 9:30 a bomb fell near Washington Place, the residence of the governor. Governor Poindexter and Secretary Charles M. Hite were there.

It was reported that the bomb killed an unidentified Chinese man across the street in front of the Schuman Carriage Co. where windows were broken.

C. E. Daniels, a welder, found a fragment of shell or bomb at South and Queen Sts. which he brought into the City Hall. This fragment weighed about a pound.

At 10:05 a. m. today Governor Poindexter telephoned to The Star-Bulletin announcing he has declared a state of emergency for the entire territory.

He announced that Edouard L. Doty, executive secretary of t he major disaster council, has been appointed director under the M-Day law's provisions.

Governor Poindexter urged all residents of Honolulu to remain off the street, and the people of the territory to remain calm.

Mr. Doty reported that all major disaster council wardens and medical units were on duty within a half hour of the time the alarm was given.

Workers employed at Pearl Harbor were ordered at 10:10 a. m. not to report at Pearl Harbor.

The mayor's major disaster council was to meet at the city hall at about 10:30 this morning

At least two Japanese planes were reported at Hawaiian department headquarters to have been shot down.

One of the planes was shot down at Ft. Kamehameha and the other back of the Wa-

Turn to Page 2, Column 1

Hundreds See City Bombed

Hundreds of Honolulans who hurried to the top of Punchbowl soon after bombs began to fall, saw spread out before them the whole panarama of surprise attack and defense.

Far off over Pearl Harbor the white sky was polka-dotted with anti-aircraft smoke.

Rolling away from the navy base were billowing clouds of ugly black smoke. Sometimes a burst of flame reddened the black source of the smoke.

Out from the silver-surfaced mouth of the harbor a flotilla of destroyers streamed to battle, smoke pouring from their stacks.

Turn to Page 2, Column 3

Schools Closed

All schools on Oahu, both public and private, will remain closed until further notice, Edward L. Doty, territorial director of civilian defense, announced at 11 a. m. today. This does not apply elsewhere in the territory.

Names of Dead and Injured

The city emergency hospital reported at 10:30 a list of 6 killed and 21 injured.

The complete list will be carried later. Here is a partial list:

Peter Lopez, 34, of 3641 Kamamalu St., was reported at 9:30 a. m. to be in serious condition from wounds in the upper abdomen.

Bernice Gouveia, 12, 2708 Kalihi St. is suffering from a mangled thigh, lacerations on the right leg and left arm.

A Portuguese girl, unidentified, 16 years old, died on arrival after puncture wounds.

Another victim who died on arrival was Frank Ohashi, 30, 1738 Kamanaki St. from puncture wounds in the chest.

Cecelia Bready, 36, Moanalua Gardens, was released from the hospital after treatment for lacerations.

Three were reported injured and one reported killed from the bomb that fell at Fort and School Sts.

Editorial

HAWAII MEETS THE CRISIS

Honolulu and Hawaii will meet the emergency of war today as Honolulu and Hawaii have met emergencies in the past—coolly, calmly and with immediate and complete support of the officials, officers and troops who are in charge.

Governor Poindexter and the army and navy leaders have called upon the public to remain calm; for civilians who have no essential business on the streets to stay off; and for every man and woman to do his duty.

That request, coupled with the measures promptly taken to meet the situation that has suddenly and terribly developed, will be needed.

Hawaii will do its part—as a loyal American territory.

In this crisis, every difference of race, creed and color will be submerged in the one desire and determination to play the part that Americans always play in crisis.

BULLETIN

Additional Star-Bulletin extras today will cover the latest developments in this war move.

COURTESY: PACIFIC MERCANTILE LIMITED, HONOLULU, HAWAII

Born In War

Lincoln's resolve reflects what veterans had in mind in 1942, when they themselves began returning wounded from the second great war. It would be several years before the ideas really jelled and they got together with their buddies to form a national organization of World War II veterans. In the meantime, they were determined that this great nation they had given their time and limbs to defend would not again be caught unprepared and that the freedoms it extended should endure. They were convinced, too, that the benefits and protections Lincoln proffered should be available in the post-war period for others like themselves, and for the widows and orphans of those who had made the supreme sacrifice.

News of the attack on Pearl Harbor (opposite) *could only hint at the destruction Japanese planes inflicted on American warships such as the U.S.S.* Shaw (above).

Collier's *made the point in its 1944 Veterans Day issue* (above) *that World War II veterans wanted their own organization. Like he did during the war, cartoonist Bill Mauldin conveyed a sense of what GIs felt* (right) *as they processed through separation centers across America.*

The beginning was desultory, if not predictable. A few loosely organized veterans clubs were formed at colleges and universities initially; then the movement mushroomed into more than 75 separate groups scattered across 30 states. *Collier's,* a leading magazine of the day, noted, "They didn't signify anything worth a second thought to state and federal politicians, to labor unions, corporations, or even to other veterans organizations."

The returnees, for their part, complained among themselves about adjustments to civilian life and the indignities thrust upon them as veterans—not to mention the way their elders and political leaders were running the country. To compound matters, discharges were swelling their ranks at a rate of 30,000 to 40,000 a month.

Soon, the 12 million soldiers, sailors, marines and coast guardsmen serving in the war would also be, in the words of *Collier's,* "12,000,000 in search of a leader."

The reference, which headlined a feature story on the various groups in the magazine's 1944 Veterans Day issue, had more than a bit of truth to it. Despite impressive numbers, these new organizations still seemed to be groping for something elusive—something they hadn't yet put together in their own minds.

Clearly, with all these people returning from the war, some sort of organized assistance on a national basis was called for. But what? The established veterans groups, like the American Legion and the Veterans of Foreign Wars (VFW), were regarded as stale and rigid, not really in tune with the interests and needs of this new generation of veterans. As one young vet put it when a question was raised about what the future would think of their activities, "Hell, we are the future!"

And what they wanted was their own organization. One of the groups, a club formed by veterans attending George Washington University and those employed by the federal government, took the lead. The American Veterans of World War II, Inc., as the organizers called themselves, began contacting other groups around the country. Each group was invited to send two delegates to a conference in Kansas City, Mo., "to discuss [the] federation of the existing veterans groups which have come out of this war."

Nine of the groups accepted and, on Dec. 9, 1944, some 70 representatives gathered at the Hotel Muehlebach in Kansas City. Reporting on the historic conference, retired Army Gen. H.C. Holdridge offered this upbeat, if not wordy, assessment: "Notwithstanding a natural initial divergence of views on minor issues, the delegates manifested a gratifying unanimity of opinion on the fundamental aims and objectives which they wished to further, and on the organization to be established to carry such objectives to a successful conclusion."

'You wuz quite a' upstart in yore day, too, sonny.'

At the conclusion of the two-day meeting, the groups merged into what United Press International described as "the only organization exclusively for discharged veterans of this war." They adopted the name American Veterans of World War II—shortened rather quickly by newspaper headline writers to AMVETS—and the motto "We Fought Together, Now Let's Build Together."

And build they did—starting with a constitution and bylaws that spelled out more than a dozen aims and purposes. AMVETS, for example, would promote world peace, preserve the American way of life and assist returning veterans in the transition from military to civilian life. These were the basic goals. Others ranged from training the country's youth "to become purposeful citizens in a democracy" to reminding the public that veterans fought "to preserve peace, liberty and democracy in their nation."

The new organization elected Elmo W. Keel, leader of the George Washington University veterans group, as its first national commander. Others considered for the post were Harold E. Stassen, former governor of Minnesota who resigned to serve in the Navy, and Col. Phil LaFolette, a member of Gen. Douglas MacArthur's staff. Both men went on to prominent military careers.

After the Kansas City conference, Keel and the others elected returned to Washington, D.C., and the headquarters office at 1507 M Street, NW. There, they began operations—with one chair, one desk and a borrowed typewriter. Albert C. Geremia, the first national executive director of AMVETS, recalls the formative weeks and months that followed: "The organization had all of the usual growing pains of adolescence, but it never swerved from its basic concepts of speaking its own mind and shouldering its hometown responsibilities."

Shortly after the meeting in Kansas City, many of the founders of AMVETS were among those invited to a dinner meeting at the White House by Eleanor Roosevelt. On hand to discuss the new organization with the First Lady were (from left) Sidney Fuher; William E. Blake; Frederick Phillips, Jr.; Carl G. Freudenberg; Andrew Kenny; Lawton Mellichamp; Joseph Motta; Floyd Cooper, Jr.; Floyd L. Williams; George E. Burke; E. Henry Miller; Albert C. Geremia; "Swede" Johnson of United Press International; Thomas H. Chunn; National Commander Elmo W. Keel; Lamarr Bailey; Rudolph Ruzicka and Claude C. Morgan. Besides Keel, others who had been in Kansas City were Blake, Freudenberg, Motta, Cooper, Williams, Burke, Miller, Geremia, Chunn, Bailey and Morgan. Founders not pictured are Glen A. Harmon, Roy E. Hughes, Paul Moody, Raymond O'Brien, Brig. Gen. Horacio C. Holdridge and Edward P. Trudell.

This building at 1507 M Street, NW, in Washington, D.C., provided the first office space for the fledgling organization. The ranks of AMVETS would soon swell with the return of thousands of GIs after the formal surrender ceremonies aboard the U.S.S. Missouri in Tokyo Bay (below) signaled the end of World War II.

During this period, AMVETS found itself competing with the older veterans groups for members. These groups—with hundreds of millions of dollars' worth of property, thousands of posts and millions of members from previous wars—signed up many new members from the ranks of World War II vets. Yet none of the groups thought that their growth would discourage the formation of an exclusively World War II organization.

When the war finally did end in 1945, the nation was jubilant. Every city, town and hamlet held parades and victory celebrations to welcome home the new veterans. The future was bright under the GI Bill of Rights, with opportunities provided to go to college and to own an affordable home. No country in the world had ever done so much for its veterans.

Beneath the euphoria, though, there were still concerns about entitlements and the country's newest and youngest veterans group worked hard to ensure that the benefits veterans earned would always be there. Membership was still the name of the game. Despite confusion, lack of funds and the usual tensions and conflicts of starting a new organization, AMVETS managed to grow. Within a year, it had more than 120 new posts and, by 1946, could boast of some 60,000 members.

The group's first formal convention took place in Chicago in October 1945. There, Jack Hardy, a Los Angeles attorney, won election as national commander—the first to be selected by grassroots delegates.

Under Hardy, the growth process shifted into high gear. Feeling the pinch for space, the national headquarters in Washington, D.C., took over an entire floor in a downtown office building at 724 9th Street, NW. And the first Auxiliary Liaison Committee was established, paving the way for the formation of the AMVETS National Auxiliary the following year in Pittsburgh.

This was just the beginning. Buoyed by the influx of new members (whose dues alone were bringing in $15,000 a month), AMVETS began to spread its political wings. With Ray Sawyer as national commander, it backed the president against labor leaders in the 1946 coal strike and successfully lobbied for the federal government to turn over management of a $5 million Washington housing project to a tenant co–op of veterans.

An early session of the National Executive Committee convenes amid austere surroundings in the office on M Street.

After the 1945 convention, National Commander Jack Hardy had the headquarters occupying an entire floor in the Victor Building (right).

But for all its clout, the young organization still lacked the "official" recognition to put it on a par with the more established veterans groups of the day. Legislation was needed, and that called for having friends on Capitol Hill. One such supporter was Francis E. Walters, Democratic congressman from Pennsylvania. Walters sponsored a bill to give AMVETS a national charter and the measure was passed unanimously in both houses of Congress.

For the World II vets, it had been a struggle to get on the map. But now they had arrived—or at least were within a presidential pen stroke of arriving. In its report on the charter legislation, the Senate Judiciary Committee believed that "such a body, organized along sound lines and for worthy purposes and broadly representative of such veterans, having demonstrated its strength and stability, is entitled to the standing and dignity which a national charter will afford."

The anticipated stature became reality when, on July 23, 1947, President Harry S. Truman signed the bill, making AMVETS the first World War II organization to be

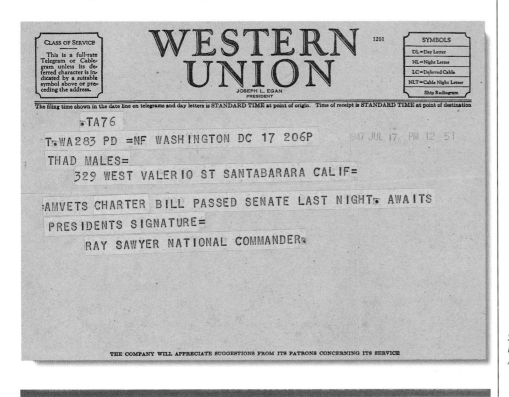

Six days after National Commander Ray Sawyer broke the good news, AMVETS had itself a charter.

14

Flanked by AMVET leaders and Rep. Francis Walters (second from left), President Truman signs Public Law 216 the organization's charter legislation; then presents the pen he used to Commander Sawyer.

chartered by Congress. More importantly, the legislation gave the group, in Sawyer's words, "legal status equal to that of the American Legion, the Veterans of Foreign Wars, the Disabled American Veterans and the United Spanish War Veterans."

But it was the president himself who put the whole matter into perspective. Mused Truman, "Were I a veteran of this war, I would prefer a veteran of World War II looking after my affairs than a veteran of some other war."

Other wars followed, each producing its own share of veterans—and its own share of potential members. When fighting broke out in Korea in 1950 and again during the Vietnam War in 1966, AMVETS prevailed on Congress to amend its charter so that veterans of these conflicts could become members. With the close of the Vietnam era in 1975, however, it would be nearly 10 years before anyone serving after that time could join.

When the membership doors did swing open in 1984—thanks to Public Law 98–304 signed by President Ronald Reagan—the way was clear for anyone who had served honorably after Sept. 15, 1940, to join. Thus, men and women on active duty became eligible and six years later, in 1990, so did national guardsmen and reservists.

The uniqueness of AMVETS was just as evident in the years following its elevation to chartered status. Indeed, in the late forties,

An amended charter made veterans of the Korean War (above) eligible for membership. President Johnson (left) signs measure allowing Vietnam veterans to become members.

President Reagan followed suit with another amendment 18 years later.

the organization became a driving force in everything from National Preparedness Day (to promote a tougher defense posture) to sponsoring Little League teams (to curb juvenile delinquency).

And membership was increasing. When Edgar C. Corry, Jr., began his term as national commander in 1947, it stood at 130,000 members. By the time the fourth national convention met in Chicago the following year, membership had jumped to more than 200,000 members in 1,700 posts across the United States and overseas.

Subordinate organizations sprang up, too. One of these was the fun–making and honor organization called the Sad Sacks, named for the famous cartoon character of World War II. The Sacks, with their own titles and bylaws, even their own auxiliary known as the Sackettes, held their first "national scrimmage" in 1947. Later,

other groups like the Sons of AMVETS and Junior AMVETS would come into being.

As AMVETS grew, so did its involvement in national affairs and public events. One of the most notable activities was the 1949 Delta Bowl in Memphis, Tenn., between Oklahoma A&M and William & Mary. The game was put on by the AMVETS National Service Foundation to supplement dues income earmarked for service work.

Over the years, the cornerstone of such work has been the free counseling and claims service provided to veterans, their dependents and survivors. Here, a small cadre of national service officers, together with their counterparts on the state level, handle thousands of claims for hospitalization, disability compensation and educational benefits. In one 12–month period, they helped to recover more than $136 million in benefits—all of which stayed in the local community.

Army Chief of Staff Omar Bradley autographs the football used in the AMVETS Delta Bowl game for National Commander Harold Keats. William & Mary beat Oklahoma A&M 20-0 before 20,000 fans on New Year's Day 1949.

The same year as the Delta Bowl, President Truman attended the national convention in Des Moines, Iowa, and dedicated the first AMVETS memorial carillon at Arlington National Cemetery. "As these bills ring out their hymns," said the president, "they will proclaim that message of faith. As long as they ring, these honored dead may rest. While faith lives, so does freedom. And while freedom lives, so does the hope of a just and lasting peace." Since then, carillons have been installed at close to 50 other sites, with funding by the National Service Foundation, which became a corporate subsidiary of AMVETS in 1948.

The Des Moines convention also ushered in Harold Russell, Mister AMVET to many and the organization's only three–time national commander. Harold, who had lost both hands in an Army training accident, went on to win two Oscars for his role in the 1946 film classic *The Best Years of Our Lives*.

By 1950, AMVETS had moved into the international arena. It became the first veterans organization to endorse the principles of the Marshall Plan (for the reconstruction of war–ravaged Europe), the establishment of the North Atlantic Treaty Organization—NATO for short—and later, the Southeast Asia Treaty Organization or SEATO. Each was subsequently adopted with AMVETS' support.

In Paris, AMVETS helped to organize the World Veterans Foundation (WVF), and even had one of its own—Elliott Newcomb, who had been national executive director—serve as the group's first secretary–general. Enthusiasm for peace ran high within this international body of ex–servicemen and for them, the United Nations was the best existing instrument for keeping it. AMVETS, under National

continued on page 24

Keats and his successor, Harold Russell (left), were on hand to greet President Truman when he arrived in Des Moines, Iowa, to address the fifth national convention in September 1949. The president, sporting his AMVETS hat, was a life member and his visit to the convention was the first ever by a chief executive. Before the year was out, he would dedicate the first AMVETS memorial carillon at Arlington Cemetery (below).

A Living Memorial

From the rolling hills of Arlington Cemetery to the quiet waters of Pearl Harbor, AMVET memorial carillons have been ringing out in honor of America's veterans for close to 50 years. Indeed, this particular program operated by the AMVETS National Service Foundation has emerged as one of the most widely recognized tributes in the country.

The carillon program dates back to 1948, when AMVETS was looking for a way to honor those who had given their lives during World War II. The organization at the time wanted something more than a marble monument—something that would serve as a "living memorial" to the sacrifices made by these men and women.

After reviewing what different veterans groups were doing in this area, AMVETS settled on the choice of a carillon as its living memorial. The tolling bells of the instrument would not only symbolize Thomas Jefferson's historic words, "Eternal vigilance is the price of liberty" but also serve as a reminder to the living not to forget that price.

The decision to use a carillon was approved at the 1948 national convention, which proposed that "AMVETS set up and perpetually maintain an electronic musical carillon in the amphitheater at Arlington near the Tomb of the Unknown Soldier as a permanent memorial for the dead of World War II."

But that was just the first step. Congressional approval would ultimately be required. To reach that point, the AMVETS proposal had to be cleared through no fewer than six government agencies. Finally, President Harry S. Truman got into the act and signed a formal resolution to Congress, recommending that the project be approved.

In October 1949, the necessary legislation was approved and sent to the president for his signature. It had taken 13 months of hard work, but the dream of having a living memorial dedicated to the nation's war dead was fast becoming reality.

Two months later, that dream was realized. On December 21, President Truman dedicated the first AMVETS memorial carillon at Arlington National Cemetery. The event was historic in other ways. For it turned out that this carillon was the first formal national monument in the cemetery dedicated to those who had given their lives in World War II.

In his address, the president uttered nine words that have since been immortalized on carillon dedication plaques throughout the nation: "... As these bells ring ... honored dead rest ... freedom lives."

With the Lincoln Memorial in the background, President Truman's motorcade (top right) crosses Memorial Bridge beneath an arch of fire truck ladders. Later in the amphitheater at Arlington National Cemetery, the president addresses those gathered for the Dec. 21, 1949, dedication of the first AMVETS memorial carillon, which is situated in the right foreground.

From top, a prayful Washington and the carillon at Freedoms Foundation; serenity at the national cemetery in Milwaukee; Jefferson Barracks, Mo., loud speakers. At right, a silent sentinel at Crownsville, Md.

The bells referred to were not the type normally associated with the term carillon. In the early instruments, such as the one at Arlington, they were compact self-contained units that were electronically operated. A carillon typically consisted of 50 such units, made of bronze bell metal, that would be struck by metal hammers. The resulting sound was a series of bell tones barely audible to the human ear. When these bell vibrations were amplified by specially designed electronic equipment, bell music was produced equal in tonal quality to that generated by mammoth traditionally cast bells.

Today, the quality is still there, only much better. The carillon, like everything else, has been refined to a point where current models operate solely on computer chips. Take the new state-of-art system donated to AMVETS National Headquarters by Schulmerich Carillons, Inc., of Sellersville, Pa. At the touch of a button, this new carillon can play up to nine musical selections automatically. And do it by remote control.

But while the Schulmerich carillon at Arlington was a far cry from this space-age model, it nevertheless was so well received that AMVETS quickly laid plans to establish an ongoing carillon program. For it seemed appropriate that wherever members of Armed Forces were buried, there, too, a carillon should be installed. With that in mind, the organization dedicated carillons at the Golden Gate National Cemetery near San Francisco, Camp Butler, Ill.; and Jefferson Barracks, Mo.

These were the first. Some of the more prominent sites include the Harry S. Truman Library in Independence, Mo.; the U.S.S. *Arizona* Memorial at Pearl Harbor; the Hoover Library in West Branch, Iowa; the John Fitzgerald Kennedy

With a memory card, Frank Huray of the National Service Foundation demonstrates how selections can be played in sequence on the latest carillon model at AMVETS National Headquarters in Lanham (below).

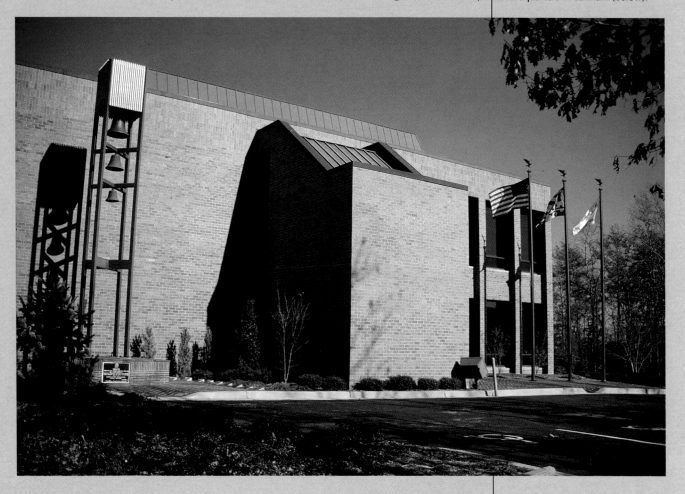

Tolling In Tribute

Housed in this semicircular colonnade are the AMVETS memorial carillon bells at the "Spirit of American Youth" Monument in the Normandy American Cemetery overlooking Omaha Beach. Other locations are:

Ft. Smith, Ark., *National Cemetery*

Bushnell, Fla., *National Cemetery*

Normandy, France
U.S. Military Cemetery

Decatur, Ga., *VA Medical Center*

Honolulu, Hawaii, *National Cemetery*

Pearl Harbor, Hawaii
U.S.S. Arizona Memorial

Camp Butler, Ill., *National Cemetery*

Chicago, Ill., *Federal Building*

Danville, Ill., *National Cemetery*

Lemont, Ill., *Mt. Vernon Memorial Estates*

Peoria, Ill., *County Courthouse*

Quincy, Ill., *Illinois Veterans Home*

Rock Island, Ill., *National Cemetery*

Marion, Ind., *National Cemetery*

West LaFayette, Ind.
Indiana Veterans Home

West Branch, Iowa, *Hoover Library*

Abilene, Kans., *Eisenhower Library*

Chalmette, La., *National Cemetery*

Jackson, La., *Louisiana War Veterans Home*

Crownsville, Md., *State Veterans Cemetery*

Lanham, Md.
AMVETS National Headquarters

Boston, Mass.
John Fitzgerald Kennedy Library

Bourne, Mass., *National Cemetery*

Augusta, Mich., *National Cemetery*

Grand Rapids, Mich.
Michigan Veterans Home

Marquette, Mich.
D.J. Jacobetti Michigan Veterans Facility

Independence, Mo.
Harry S. Truman Library

Jefferson Barracks, Mo.
National Cemetery

Springfield, Mo., *National Cemetery*

Buffalo, N.Y., *Buffalo Naval Park*

Buffalo, N.Y., *VA Medical Center*

Calverton, N.Y., *National Cemetery*

Montrose, N.Y., *VA Medical Center*

Northport, N.Y., *VA Medical Center*

Fayetteville, N.C., *VA Medical Center*

Salisbury, N.C., *National Cemetery*

Dayton, Ohio, *National Cemetery*

Sandusky, Ohio
Ohio Soldiers and Sailors Home

Fort Gibson, Okla., *National Cemetery*

Eagle Point, Oreg., *National Cemetery*

Manila, Republic of the Philippines
U.S. Military Cemetery

Indiantown Gap, Pa., *National Cemetery*

Valley Forge, Pa., *Freedoms Foundation*

Florence, S.C., *National Cemetery*

Houston, Tex., *National Cemetery*

Salt Lake City, Utah
State Capitol Building

Arlington, Va., *National Cemetery*

Quantico, Va., *National Cemetery*

Milwaukee, Wis., *National Cemetery*

From top, dedicating the carillon at the Eisenhower Library; playing the instrument at Salt Lake City; National Commander Robert Medairos (left) and Department of New York Commander Benjamin Delucci participating in the carillon dedication at the VA medical center in Montrose, N.Y.

Library in Boston; the Eisenhower Library in Abilene, Kans.; the state capitol building in Salt Lake City; and Freedoms Foundation at Valley Forge.

On July 4, 1976, a carillon was installed at AMVETS National Headquarters, then housed on Rhode Island Avenue in Washington, D.C. After the headquarters moved to Lanham, another carillon was dedicated on Aug. 14, 1985. This particular carillon—known as the AMVETS National Memorial Carillon—is symbolic of the program as a whole.

An added dimension is the AMVETS National Memorial Roster maintained in the chapel at national headquarters. AMVET members and supporters may enroll a deceased family member, relative or friend who served honorably in the armed services. The bells of the national memorial carillon are then programmed to toll at specific times in honor of those enrolled on the roster.

In the beginning, the national program was directed by AMVETS, but as the years passed and more money was needed to finance it, the National Service Foundation began to provide the monies to purchase and install carillons. Nowadays, AMVET departments that request installation of a carillon share the cost.

To date, 20 states have one or more carillon sites, with there being 48 sites worldwide. At each of them, an AMVETS memorial carillon conveys the same message—one captured in these elegant words spoken by Gov. George Dewey Clyde of Utah: "Each time that this carillon rings out music, it will turn our minds to the memory of the men for whom it is played, and the gratitude which we owe them for making the ultimate sacrifice in order to preserve our American heritage."

—Dick Flanagan and Tonya Swann

The 37th AMVETS memorial carillon was dedicated Jan. 27, 1986, at the National Memorial Cemetery of the Pacific in Honolulu, Hawaii. The Punchbowl, as the cemetery is commonly called, is visited each year by the AMVETS national commander and Auxiliary president, who together lay a wreath there as well as at the U.S.S. Arizona Memorial, where another carillon was dedicated on Memorial Day 1960.

continued from page 17

Commander Marshall E. Miller, actively participated in the work of the UN and was one of the non–governmental agencies accredited by it. After 1982, though, the organization ceased being an active member of the WVF.

In 1952, AMVETS dedicated its first headquarters in downtown Washington. The four–story brick building at 1710 Rhode Island Avenue, NW, had been the site of the wedding of President William Howard Taft's niece. Fourteen years later, when Ralph E. Hall was national commander, a second national headquarters would be built on the same site and dedicated by President Lyndon B. Johnson.

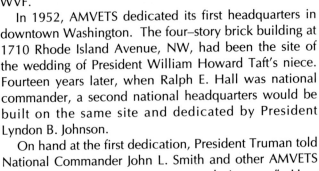

On hand at the first dedication, President Truman told National Commander John L. Smith and other AMVETS that "your organization is young and vigorous." He also confirmed what many observers already knew. "I've noticed," said the president, "that the AMVETS do not approach things from the narrow standpoint of the immediate interests of veterans. Instead, you're looking at things in terms of the general public interest."

That's part of the reason. The other part had to do with the way AMVETS operat-

AMVETS influence was felt in the World Veterans Foundation, where Elliott Newcomb (right) *served as secretary general, and in the UN.*

President Truman prepares to dedicate the first headquarters on Rhode Island Avenue in Washington, D.C. President Johnson (above) *did the honors after a second headquarters was built there in 1966. Note bust at right (see page 48).*

ed (and still does): always from the supposition that the veteran will ultimately benefit from any measure that benefits the nation. By developing workable proposals to help the country as a whole, AMVET leaders have been able to address issues in the light of their surrounding circumstances. In 1953, for example, when budget reductions threatened the Veterans Administration medical program, AMVETS gave Congress and the president a 9-point "economy" package to save the government as much as $90 million without reducing the quality of veterans health care. Eventually, eight of the nine points were either enacted into law or carried out by various administrative rulings within VA.

Meanwhile, in its own backyard, National Commander Dominick L. Strada had initiated a "gold brick" drive to pay off the mortgage on the national headquarters. By the time AMVETS reached its 10th year of operation under Henry J. Mahady, *Collier's* was calling it "the largest and most successful of the new veterans organizations." And with good reason. From the early days when crates served as chairs, AMVETS had grown, not only in size but also in stature.

Many things contributed. In 1954, AMVETS unveiled what has come to be called the "Veterans Oscar," a silver replica of the World War II G.I. helmet awarded to outstanding Americans for their exceptional achievements (*page 28*). National Commander Rufus H. Wilson presented the first such Silver Helmet Award to General of the Army George C. Marshall for "his enormous contributions to the United States in war and peace."

In recent years, the award has been given at a special banquet, held annually in conjunction with the AMVETS spring National Executive Committee meeting, to recognize excellence in such fields as Americanism, defense, rehabilitation, congressional service and peace. On occasion, Gold Helmet Awards have also been given for outstanding accomplishment. The first was presented to President Johnson in 1968 by then National Commander Anthony J. Caserta; the most recent to President George Bush in 1992.

The same drive to contribute seems to have fueled AMVETS' own efforts in the very areas where it was recognizing the achievements of others. Take the matter of

National Commander Anthony Caserta presents the first Gold Helmet Award to President Johnson. Twenty-four years later in a similar White House ceremony, National Commander James Singler makes the presentation to President George Bush. Mrs. Bush has just received the AMVETS Auxiliary Humanitarian Award from National President Dorothy Bull.

defense. Throughout its history, AMVETS has continually emphasized how important it is to keep America strong. Whether urging universal military training or dis-

continued on page 27

In the Beginning

For 20 years, Lester Spear worked as an AMVETS service officer at the VA Regional Office in his hometown of New York City. A resident today of Wheaton, Md., he recounts here his entry into the service officer program during the early years of AMVETS.

I had not planned to train as an AMVETS national service officer since I had been notified I could matriculate at Colorado State University. This was 1946 and I received the notice about two months before I was to begin my studies at Colorado State. In the meantime, I had already joined AMVETS and was attending post meetings at the Bronx County Courthouse. At one of those meetings, Larry Marshall, a lawyer and an active AMVETS member, advised me that the organization had several openings for applicants to train as national service officers. He suggested that I apply. To keep my options open, I decided to, even though I knew very little about the job. At any rate, the Veterans Administration gave the test and soon after, I was informed that I had passed.

Within two weeks, I received word from National Service Director James Tate that I had been accepted as a candidate. Now I had to choose between Colorado State University or the National Service Officers' School at American University, which was sponsored by the Disabled American Veterans. The decision was not too difficult. I decided to attend the service officers school where, under Public Law 16, I would receive a stipend each month plus whatever AMVETS would pay. I would also be guaranteed a job at the end of the course, which was appealing. Colorado State did not provide this incentive.

Initially, there were four AMVETS candidates selected to attend. Even though two candidates dropped out early in the program, Rufus Wilson and I remained. We completed the six-month course and received a full-year of college credits. Jack Hardy, the first elected commander, congratulated us on our achievements and off we went for our on-the-job training. Rufus went to Detroit for six months and I went to Pass-A-Grille, Fla., for six months. Our next assignment was Atlanta for six months where we trained under the Georgia Director of Veterans Affairs Arthur Cheetham.

Ray Sawyer appointed Clarence Adamy as the first national service director. He had been sponsored by the DAV and was a fellow student of Rufus and myself in Class 8 at the service officers school. Adamy appointed Rufus assistant national service director, while I chose to establish the service office at the VA regional office in New York City, my hometown.

New York State Commander Harry Borsher and Frank Scarane, national executive committeeman, were instrumental in having me assigned to the New York City office of the VA. That was 1947 and for about 20 years, I worked at the New York regional office with the assistance of Stephen Sikely who was also director of the service office at the regional office in Newark, N.J.

One of my highlights as a service officer in New York was arranging meetings as well as the awarding of the National Rehabilitation Award to Bernard Baruch, advisor to President Truman and Franklin D. Roosevelt.

continued from page 25

couraging public apathy, the organization could always be counted on to take a stand.

Early in the fifties, AMVETS pilot-tested a blood-tagging program and, subsequently, took the lead in the nation's civil defense efforts, including the construction of home shelters. For almost 10 years, the organization hammered away at the importance of preparedness. Finally, in May 1961, President John F. Kennedy assigned responsibility for civil defense to the secretary of defense and established the Office of Emergency Planning. National Commander Edwin P. Fifielski's civil defense caravan, complete with model fallout shelter, had traveled 45,000 miles through 37 states to spread the word. Some AMVET posts even built shelters as models for their communities.

Whether such single-mindeness is an inherent AMVETS trait is arguable. What people do know, and will tell you, is that the group's national commanders have never shied from speaking out on issues. This willingness to go one-on-one with controversy could take the form of endorsement, or condemnation. Like the time a fiery Harold Russell came to President Truman's defense over the latter's dismissal of General MacArthur during the Korean War.

As national commander, Russell felt that AMVETS' mandated policies gave him ample justification to endorse the commander-in-chief's right to recall any officer who was not carrying out orders. Many AMVET members felt otherwise and came storming into Washington, prepared to give Russell a piece of their minds.

When it came time to state his case, Harold mounted the rostrum, deadly serious and adamant about the position he had taken. One by one he made his points, punctuating each with violent thrusts of his hooks on the lectern. Perspiration streamed down his face as staff members seated nearby kept a constant chain of handkerchiefs moving toward him. By the time the speech was finished, those in attendance would agree they had witnessed one of the most dramatic presentations in AMVETS history.

The decade also saw the advent of various scholarship programs. In 1952, AMVETS began providing, through its memorial scholarship program, education grants to the sons and daughters of deceased and disabled veterans. A White House visit by National

continued on page 34

The Civil Defense Caravan prepares to hit the road from Boston's Old North Church. National Commander Harold Russell (center) stood his ground on the MacArthur dismissal. National Commander Rudolph Pesata made it a point to brief President Eisenhower on the memorial scholarship program.

The Veterans Oscar

For those in attendance, the moment was a particularly poignant one. General of the Army George C. Marshall had just been presented with the first AMVETS Silver Helmet Award, in recognition of his contributions as a soldier, statesman and American. The occasion, a banquet in Washington commemorating the organization's 10th anniversary, was marked with smiles and tears.

Holding the gleaming helmet, a replica of those worn by GIs in World War II, the misty-eyed Marshall stood erect as he told his audience about an unfulfilled ambition. "It has always been a matter of keen regret to me," confided the old soldier, "that I was not able to be more closely associated with you in the great dangers [at the fighting front during World War II]."

Since that inaugural presentation in 1954, the AMVETS Silver Helmet Award has over the years acquired a well-deserved reputation as the most prestigious of all veterans organization awards. Indeed, the award, which symbolizes Marshall's World War II leadership, has come to be known as the "Veterans Oscar."

In recent years, the Silver Helmet Awards ceremony has become an annual event to recognize excellence and outstanding accomplishments in such fields as Americanism, defense, rehabilitation, congressional service and peace. Early annual awards in these areas were the forerunners of today's Silver Helmet. To date, more than 260 awards of the Silver Helmet have been made to deserving individuals who "stepped forward to make a real difference in the world about them." Honored, too, have been special programs, projects and even entire groups of people.

Nominations for the Silver Helmet Awards originate with individual AMVET members and AMVET posts around the country and are endorsed by the respective state AMVETS honors and awards committees prior to the AMVETS National Convention in August. The AMVETS National Honors and Awards Committee, composed of all past national commanders and the last five "AMVET of the Year" awardees, reviews the nominations and makes recommendations to the convention, which determines the recipients.

The Silver Helmet Awards Banquet is held annually in conjunction with an AMVETS National Executive Committee meeting. In addition to AMVET members, the audience includes cabinet members, senators, representatives and military officials who come to pay tribute to the recipients of the award and AMVETS.

The award to Marshall (left) set in motion an annual event renowned for the personages it attracted.

This occasion is also the time when the AMVETS Auxiliary presents its annual Humanitarian Award. Presented since 1976, the award goes to "an outstanding American who serves our country in peace as in war; who builds and maintains the welfare of the United States of America toward lasting prosperity and peace for all its inhabitants." The first recipient was Corinne "Lindy" C. Boggs.

Another special award is the Gold Helmet, instituted in 1968 to recognize exceptional contributions made by a president of the United States. The award is treated as one given by the national commander of a major veterans organization to the president as commander-in-chief of the Armed Forces. President Lyndon B.

AMERICANISM		
1952— James H. Duff	1951— Albert C. Geremia	1958— Mary Switzer
1953— Bernard M. Baruch	1952— Robert A. Burrell	1960— Douglas D. Toffe
1954— Spyros P. Skouras	1953— John M. Murphy	1961— Dwight D. Guilfo
1955— G. Mennen Williams	1954— Edgar C. Corry	1962— William S. Middle
1956— John C. Brogen	1955— William E. Murphy	1963— Winifred Overho
1957— Phil Silvers	1956— William B. Whitman	1964— Nicholas J. Ogane
1958— Harry S. Truman	1957— Martin D. Schwartz	1967— William J. Driver
1959— Van Cliburn and	1958— Harold Berc	1968— Richard Bush
Rafer L. Johnson	1959— Herbert Bennett	1969— Henry Viscardi, Jr
1960— Herbert S. Hoover	1960— William Kipp	1970— William P. McCa
1961— LeRoy Collins	1962— Edward Gallagher	1971— Criss Cole
1962— J. Edgar Hoover	1963— D. Arthur Connelly	1972— Albert P. Russo
1963— George Meany	1964— Doris Bradley	1973— Harold Russell
1964— Carl Sanders	1965— Ralph Hall	1974— Irving M. Levine
1965— Charles Rhyne	1966— Anthony J. Caserta	1975— Richard L. Roude
1966— Frances P. Bolton	1968— George B. Kennedy, Jr.	1976— John L. Quigley
1967— Kenneth D. Wells	1969— Berge Avadanian	1977— Odell W. Vaughr
1968— Walter Winchell	1970— Joseph R. Sanson	1978— John D. Chase
1969— Richard Cardinal Cushing	1971— Frank J. Scarane	1979— Jack J. Dack
1970— Richard ("Red") Skelton	1972— Fred J. Tonnemacher	1980— Rocky Bleier
1971— Paul Powell	1973— Joseph B. Porter	1981— Dennis R. Wyant
1972— John Wayne	1974— Julius R. Pollatschek	1982— Jim Martinson
1973— Johnny Mann	1975— Robert Martin	1983— Johnny Thomas C
1974— Joe DiMaggio	1976— Catherine C. Moore	1985— Raymond Colem
1975— Elliot L. Richardson	1977— William E. Brown, Sr.	1986— Pete Wheeler
1976— Richard J. Daley	1978— John B. Engberg II	1987— A. Malachi Mixo
1977— Kathryn ("Kate") E. Smith	1979— Herbert Hayes	1988— Paul Stanley Sher
1978— Robert W. Miller	1980— James L. Singler	1989— Philip H. Viall
1979— Richard G. Bucksar	1981— Earl B. Wright	1990— James S. Brady
1980— Hugh O'Brian	1982— Edgar Williams	1991— William A. Demb
1982— Thomas A. Murphy	1983— E. Cecil Keller	1992— Ted Leszkiewicz
1983— Harry Lee	1984— Bill White	1993— Dante Spagnolo
1984— Dom and Carol DeLuise	1985— William ("Bill") D. Hill	1994— Ken Smith
1985— Lee A. Iacocca	1987— Manuel Toledo	
1986— James H. Cohen	1988— James Jay	**CONGRESSIONAL**
1987— Ken Lipke	1989— Raymond Hess	1952— Olin E. Teague
1988— Lee Greenwood	1990— Pete Valdez	1953— Edith Nourse Rog
1989— Richard Michel	1991— Daniel J. Caputo	1956— William H. Ayres
1990— Kevin Dobson	1992— Joseph B. Gresham	1958— Harry F. Byrd
1991— Arthur M. Kaplan	1993— Thomas Barr	1959— Edwin Ross Adai
1992— Gerald E. Radcliffe	1994— Joseph T. Kolano	1960— H. Erwin Mitche
1993— James Quillen		1962— Everett M. Dirkse
1994— Peter Coors	**REHABILITATION**	1963— Edmund S. Musk
	1952— Arthur S. Abramson	1964— Estes C. Kefauver
AMVET OF THE YEAR	1953— Henry J. Kessler	1965— Clement J. Zablo
1948— Ray Sawyer	1954— Howard Rusk	1966— Peter W. Rodino
1949— Prentics G. Smith	1955— Karl A. Menninger	1967— John W. McCorn
1950— Paul A. Kern	1956— Russell C. Williams	1968— Edward W. Broo
	1957— Melvin J. Maas	1969— Wilbur D. Mills

Johnson, who had received the Silver Helmet Defense Award eight years before when he was Majority leader of the Senate, was selected as the first Gold Helmet recipient. Since then, Presidents Nixon, Ford, Reagan and Bush have been so honored.

Over time, the physical appearance of both the Silver Helmet and the Humanitarian Award has changed. Yet, like time-honored institutions, the awards themselves are immutable—their cosmetic changes being but variations on a common, but noble, theme. That of recognizing the service of others with the highest honor an organization can bestow *(below)*.

)— William Jennings Bryan Dorn	1983— James C. Donahue	1966— Maxwell D. Taylor
◀— Gerald R. Ford	1984— Donald M. Skinder	1967— U.S. Armed Forces
2— Roman C. Pucinski	1985— Harry N. Walters	1968— Lewis B. Hershey
3— John P. Saylor	1986— Elizabeth Hanford Dole	1969— William C. Westmoreland
4— Margaret M. Heckler	1987— Mack Fleming	1970— Creighton W. Abrams
5— Hugh D. Scott	1988— Edward Rose	1971— Melvin R. Laird
6— Barry M. Goldwater	1990— Joan Giannini	1972— F. Edward Hebert
7— Strom Thurmond	1991— Thomas F. Higgins	1973— David Packard
8— Jack F. Kemp	1992— Thomas C. Doherty	1974— Henry M. Jackson
9— Lucien N. Nedzi	1993— Anthony Cinquanta	1975— John P. Flynn
0— Herbert Ray Roberts	1994— Henry David Hardt	1976— Daniel J. ("Chappie") James, Jr.
— Alan Cranston		
2— Robert J. Dole	**PEACE**	1985— Caspar Weinberger
3— Howard H. Baker	1951— Paul Hoffman	1991— Colin L. Powell
4— G.V. ("Sonny") Montgomery	1952— John Foster Dulles	1992— Norman Schwarzkopf
5— Alan K. Simpson	1953— Elliott Newcomb	
6— John Paul Hammerschmidt	1954— All U.S. servicemen and women and John E. Peurifoy	**SPECIAL AWARD**
7— Marvin Leath		1961— Robert ("Bob") Hope
8— Edward P. Boland	1955— Walter F. George	1962— Astronaut Team of Project Mercury
9— Gerald B. Solomon	1958— Dag Hammarskjold	1963— TELSTAR
0— Chalmers P. Wylie	1959— Dwight D. Eisenhower	1964— Edward A. McDermott
2— W.G. "Bill" Hefner	1960— Richard M. Nixon	1965— Oliver E. Meadows
3— Michael Bilirakis	1961— Henry Cabot Lodge	1966— Ralph W. Yarborough and Richard K. Mellon
— Bob Stump	1962— Eleanor Roosevelt	1967— Martha Raye
	1963— Lucius D. Clay	1968— George E. Arneman
CIVIL SERVANT	1964— John F. Kennedy	1969— P.E. ("Gene") Howard
— John Macy	1965— Adlai E. Stevenson	1970— Theodore M. Hesburgh
— William C. Hull	1966— Ralph J. Bunche	1971— Dodge Division, Chrylser Corporation; United Service Organizations, Inc.; Danny Thomas; and Frank Blair
— U.E. Baughman	1968— Arthur J. Goldberg	
— Homer E. Newell	1969— W. Averell Harriman	
— Hugh Bradley	1970— Apollo Eleven Crew	
— James P. McShane	1971— Pope Paul VI	
— L.J. Andolsek	1972— Henry Kissinger	
— Reed Harris	1973— Joseph J. Sisco	1972— Dominick L. Strada and Walter E. Washington
— Edward L. Omohundro	1975— Michael ("Mike") J. Mansfield	
— Robert Hampton	1981— Pope John Paul II	1973— Raymond Burr
— Irene Parson	1987— F. Branford Morse	1974— Peter J. Brennan
— Gordon R. Elliott	1989— George Shultz	1975— Gordon Sinclair
— James E. Johnson		1977— Rick Monday and Ralph Nader
— Aladino A. Gavazzi	**DEFENSE**	1978— Sig Sakowicz and Earl B. Wright
— Joseph P. Yeldell	1959— Stuart Symington	
— Jayne Baker Spain	1960— Lyndon B. Johnson	
— William J. Usery, Jr.	1961— Leo A. Hoegh	1979— Aloysius Schwartz and Lori Cox
— Dorothy L. Starbuck	1962— Hyman G. Rickover	
— William F. Connors	1963— Robert S. McNamara	
— Dorothy S. Looney	1964— Curtis E. LeMay	
— Andrew V. Schally	1965— Carl Vinson	

President Dwight Eisenhower (top) was the 1959 Peace Award recipient, while President Harry Truman was presented the Americanism Award in 1958 by National Commander Stuart Satullo. Comedian Phil Silvers had received the award the previous year from National Commander Dominic Strada, who received a Special Award in 1972.

Silver Helmet Award is a registered trademark name of the American Veterans of World War II, Korea and Vietnam (AMVETS).

1980— Raymond J. Costanzo	1989— Jimmy Crum	1982— Russell C. Barbor
1982— Frank Sinatra	1993— Ralph E. Hall	1988— Sam Nunn
1983— Ferdinand Marcos	1994— Paul C. Welsh	1990— Francis R. Gerard
1986— Robert T. Secrest and		
The McDonald's	**MEMORIAL**	**SPECIAL GOLD HELMET**
Corporation	1993— Silent Crew of the	1968— Lyndon B. Johnson
1987— Sister Maria Veronica	U.S.S. *Arizona*	1970— Richard M. Nixon
1987— Special Olympics	(Posthumous)	1977— Gerald R. Ford
1988— Frank Harden and		1982— Ronald Reagan
Jackson Weaver	**MERITORIOUS ACHIEVEMENT**	1992— George Bush

Sheriff Harry Lee of Louisiana (top) holds the Americanism Award given to him in 1983. Seven years later, actor Kevin Dobson received the award from PNC James Singler, selected as AMVET of the Year in 1980. Rep. Chalmers Wylie receives the 1991 Congressional Award from PNC Paul Welsh, who was honored with a Special Award in 1994.

AUXILIARY HUMANITARIAN	
— Corrine ("Lindy") Boggs	1984— John McCain
— Mrs. Spencer Tracy	1985— Bill Kurtis
— Roy Rogers and	1986— Nancy D. Reagan
Dale Evans	1987— Jack Klugman
— Eunice Shriver	1988— Margaret "Peggy" Say
— Martha Roundtree	1990— Abigail Van Buren
— Dorothy Fuldheim	1991— Donald W. Benson
— Joy K. Ufima	1992— Barbara Bush
— Danny Kaye	1993— Rosalyn Carter
	1994— Marlo Thomas

At top, Lee Greenwood gives a thumbs up after receiving the Americanism Award in 1988. Peace Award Recipient Henry Cabot Lodge (left) and comedian Bob Hope, who received a Special Award, share a laugh with National Commander Harold Russell at the 1961 Silver Helmet Awards Luncheon (center). Roy Rogers and wife Dale Evans were selected to receive the Auxiliary's third Humanitarian Award in 1978.

Twenty years after Robert Gomulinski (above) was national commander, DE was a program in need of a sponsor until Toyota came on board in 1992. A year later, the pilot of the AMVETS-Toyota U.S.A. Safe Driving Challenge was run in Natick, Mass., under National Commander James Kenney (right), with the national finals being held in Indianapolis in 1994.

Navy Secretary Franke thought AMVETS was the logical choice to erect the wall in the memorial atop the sunken Arizona.

continued from page 27

Commander Rudolph G. Pesata to brief President Dwight D. Eisenhower on the program boosted its visibility until, today, it distributes some $60,000 annually.

Later, in 1958, when President Eisenhower called on private organizations to support science education, AMVETS National Commander Stuart J. Satullo was among the first to respond. Accepting the first AMVETS science scholarship at a White House ceremony, Ike said, "The AMVETS program fulfills one of the highest purposes to which a veterans group can devote itself—that of providing an opportunity of advanced education for young men and women." The following year, AMVETS added a scholarship program for physical education study to promote physical fitness. Dr. Winston E. Burdine, national commander at the time, also served on the President's Advisory Committee on Physical Fitness.

The organization's commitment to youth was not limited to just the classroom. Something had to be done about the nation's highways to make them safer. The answer was the AMVETS National Safety Program, established in 1957 in cooperation with the Dodge Division of Chrysler Corporation. Out of it grew the AMVETS-Dodge Driver Excellence Program, a national competition for high school students who completed driver education courses. Launched during A. Leo Anderson's term as national commander, the DE program—which emphasized defensive driving and awarded scholarships to the winners—was temporarily shelved in 1989 when Dodge withdrew. Three years later, it emerged again—after much internal debate—as the AMVETS-Toyota U.S.A., Inc., Safe Driving Challenge Program.

It was during this period, too, that AMVETS became heavily involved in the development of the Korean G.I. Bill of Rights. In fact, the organization ended up devising ways to administer the bill to save the government money without reducing the benefits. So significant were the AMVET contributions that Congressman Olin Teague of Texas, ranking member of the House Veterans Affairs Committee at the time (and later its chairman), didn't hesitate to tell people that "AMVETS had more to do with this bill than any other organization."

The same can be said of the group's efforts on behalf of the *U.S.S. Arizona* Memorial. In 1947, the Pacific War Memorial Commission was authorized to establish the memorial by raising needed funds from the public. Although the memorial was incomplete, AMVETS volunteered to install a carillon at the site. Secretary of the Navy W.B. Franke then suggested that the organization might want to also erect a memorial wall bearing the names of the 1,102 men who went down with the gallant ship. National Commander Harold T. Berc committed AMVETS to raising the money for the wall, which it did.

From the original artist's concept (left), *the memorial wall took shape until, in 1962, it was dedicated, with National Commander Edward Fifielski laying a wreath in honor of those who had perished.*

While dedicating the carillon, Berc learned that $250,000 was still needed to complete the memorial. He reasoned that if the 1,102 crewmen had been separately interred, their individual VA burial allowances would more than total the amount needed. When Eisenhower heard this, he authorized AMVETS to publicly announce his support of a completion appropriation.

By 1983, 21 years after the original dedication, the names on the memorial wall were being eroded away by the elements. AMVETS again would come up with the necessary funds ($50,000)—this time under National Commander Robert Martin—to take the wall apart and totally replace it, including all the hardware. A year later, the new wall was dedicated by National Commander Robert T. Wilbraham. In 1991, a special memorial room was dedicated to the U.S.S. *Arizona* at AMVETS National Headquarters, with a memorial award of the Silver Helmet subsequently going to its crew.

Impressive as these and other initiatives were, problems arose in the early sixties. Less than 10 years after Harry Truman had described AMVETS as being *vigorous*, its membership and finances were anything but that.

The National Committee on Reevaluation reported to the 1961 convention that membership had dropped to 60,000, the same as it was in 1946. The committee noted further that roughly half a million members had been recruited over the years, but that AMVETS was "signing them up one year and losing them the next."

More disconcerting was the fact that income had exceeded operating expenses by only $2,400 in the first 15 years of operation. The organization simply couldn't go on like that. Bluntly put, AMVETS would be bankrupt in two years' time.

continued on page 44

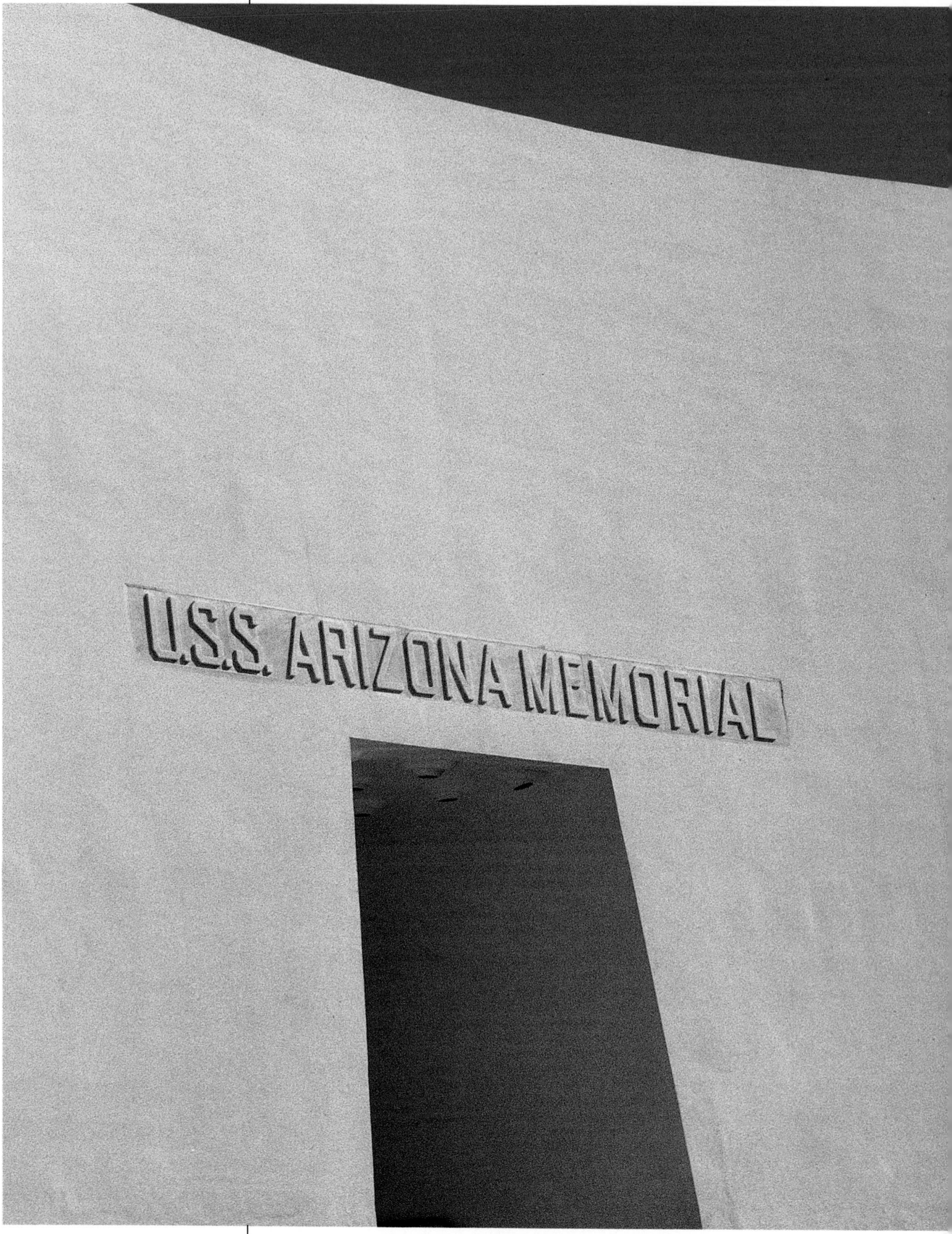
U.S.S. ARIZONA MEMORIAL

A Wall For BB-39

"**W**hether the country knows it or not, we are at war." So said Adm. Harold R. "Betty" Stark, chief of naval operations, after a German U-boat sank the destroyer U.S.S. *Ruben James* in the North Atlantic on Oct. 31, 1941, claiming 115 lives. Less than two months later, the Japanese would attack Pearl Harbor and force America to face the grim reality of war. For many Americans, December 7 marked a change in the world as they knew it.

It also marked the beginnings of AMVETS, and subsequently its long association with perhaps the best known war memorial in the world—the U.S.S. *Arizona* Memorial. The story of the memorial is one of a reluctant Congress being prodded by a determined veterans group to provide a fitting shrine for those who gave their lives on the U.S.S. *Arizona* (BB-39).

Of all the battleships hit during the Japanese attack, the *Arizona* was the only one to receive major bomb damage. The bottom of the gallant ship was blown out and she "blew up like a million Fourth of Julys," recalled a witness who saw a torpedo speed under his repair ship, the U.S.S. *Vestal*, and into the huge dreadnought moored alongside.

The campaign for a memorial to honor the dead of the *Arizona*, and all who died at Pearl Harbor that day, began when Public Law 85–344 was approved Mar. 15, 1958, authorizing the secretary of the Navy to construct such a shrine, where the names of the 1,177 who died aboard that morning would be inscribed on a marble wall. AMVETS seemed to be the logical choice to undertake the funding of the wall and Secretary of the Navy William B. Franke suggested the project to National Commander Harold T. Berc of Chicago. Berc accepted the challenge for AMVETS to raise the $15,000 needed to commission the engraving of the wall. On Memorial Day 1960, during the dedication of an AMVETS memorial carillon aboard a new platform over the *Arizona*, he presented the Pacific War Memorial Commission with a $9,000 check toward construction of the memorial wall, with the promise of more to come.

Building costs for the entire shrine were estimated to be more than half-a-million dollars, but the funds originally appropriated by Congress amounted to only $150,000. The Hawaii legislature allocated $100,000, but the bulk—amounting to almost $275,000—was expected to be raised by public donations. The Pacific War Memorial Commission, chaired by H. Tucker Gratz, began raising funds for the *Arizona* Memorial on Dec. 7, 1957. But not all went smoothly.

The Arizona *was a 30,600-ton battleship—the third vessel bearing that name. Commanded by Capt. John D. MacDonald with 55 officers and 860 crewmen, she was commissioned on Oct. 17, 1916, and eight years later, joined the Battle Fleet of the West Coast.*

Devastated by an aerial torpedo and seven bombs, the Arizona sinks in a shroud of smoke beneath the shallow water of Pearl Harbor. The Japanese attack damaged or sunk 21 U.S. ships and accounted for more than 2,400 people dead or missing.

By the time Commander Berc returned to Washington from the carillon dedication, the project needed another $200,000 to be completed. Berc argued for the appropriation, pointing out "it was less than the sum of the $250 veterans' burial allowance which would have been payable to each of the men who still rests inside the *Arizona*."

In response, Berc received pledges from both President Eisenhower and President-Elect Kennedy—himself an active AMVET member—that they would support legislation authorizing Congress to use public monies to finish the shrine. Sen. Hiram Fong of Hawaii then introduced S. 3789 on June 30, 1960, to allow final funding from public monies. Approval of the necessary funding was assured on Aug. 9, 1961, when Sen. Richard Russell of Georgia, chairman of the Senate Armed Services Committee, acceded to AMVETS' demands.

During the struggle for congressional support, prominent Americans donated their talents to the project. Elvis Presley raised $67,000 on a March, 1961, show at the Pearl Harbor Naval Base and, together with his manager, Col. Tom Parker, gave

Before the Arizona *Memorial was built, this simple platform provided access to the sunken ship.*

National Commander Harold Berc presents Navy Secretary William Franke with a replica of carillon bells symbolizing AMVETS' promise to install a carillon at the site of the Arizona. Later, aboard the platform for the dedication of the carillon, he makes a presentation of funds for construction of the memorial wall.

Berc shakes hands with President Eisenhower, who threw support behind legislation authorizing the use of public funds to finish construction of the memorial.

According to designer Alfred Preis, the Arizona Memorial "sags in the center but stands strong and vigorous in the ends, expressing initial defeat and ultimate victory."

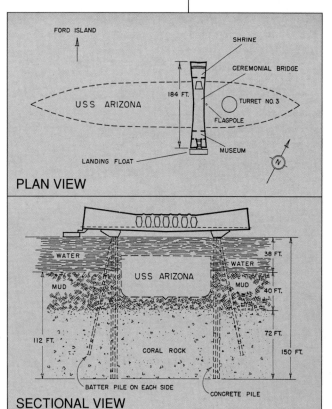

PLAN VIEW

FORD ISLAND

SHRINE

CEREMONIAL BRIDGE

184 FT.

USS ARIZONA

TURRET NO. 3

FLAGPOLE

MUSEUM

LANDING FLOAT

N

SECTIONAL VIEW

WATER

38 FT.

WATER

USS ARIZONA

MUD

MUD

40 FT.

112 FT.

72 FT.

CORAL ROCK

150 FT.

BATTER PILE ON EACH SIDE

CONCRETE PILE

an additional $25,000. Ralph Edwards, host of TV's "This Is Your Life," came up with another $80,000 during a special filming of the show at Pearl Harbor.

There were others, too, outside the AMVET family, who rallied in support of the shrine. Students at Roberts Junior High School in Medford, Mass., for example, raised more than $800 for the wall, selling gift-wrapping ribbons and greeting cards. Elsewhere, eighth graders at the Marquis de LaFayette school in Elizabeth, N.J., designed and sold "Freedom Shares" to collect money for the memorial.

Construction of the U.S.S. *Arizona* Memorial began in July 1960 and was completed on May 25, 1962. Designed by architect Alfred Preis as an enclosed bridge spanning the sunken hull of the *Arizona*, the 21-foot-high, 185-foot-long white shrine can accommodate close to 200 people. It ranges in width from 27 feet in the center, to 36 feet at either end. The structure is supported by two concrete girders weighing 250 tons each and resting on prestressed concrete piles.

Visitors entering the memorial on the Waikiki side can observe colorful tropical fish swimming beneath the surface in waters where oil still seeps from the rusting hull. A flag pole attached to the ship rises alongside the structure. The Ewa side of the memorial houses the marble wall with the names of the those who died in the attack, 1,102 of whom are still entombed below.

AMVETS National Commander Edwin P. Fifielski of Chicago, who led the 21-member AMVETS delegation to Pearl Harbor for the memorial's dedication, said it was "the fulfillment of a five-year struggle by AMVETS to help make this shrine a living reality." Also on hand was Anne Hall, AMVETS Auxiliary national president from the Department of Massachusetts, representing the close to 15,000 women of the Auxiliary.

The dedication ceremony on Memorial Day, May 30, 1962, began at 9:30 a.m. when two formations of jets from Marine Attack Squadron 212 screamed overhead. About 1,000 people were present—800 on nearby Ford Island and another 200 onboard the *Arizona*.

National Commander Robert Martin, shown here with wife Earlene, led the drive to fund a new memorial wall. Below, National Commander Edwin Fifielski and Auxiliary President Anne Hall are joined by Commission Chairman Tucker Gratz (left) and Rep. Olin Teague at the 1962 dedication.

Rep. Olin E. Teague, the powerful chairman of the House Veterans Affairs Committee and himself a highly decorated World War II veteran, delivered the keynote address. In his remarks, Teague noted that "as far as I'm concerned, AMVETS—as a national organization—did more to complete this memorial in cooperation with the Pacific War Memorial Commission than any other group that I know of in the country."

Colonel Parker cabled commission chairman Gratz the same day, saying, "Wish Elvis and I could be there for the big moment you are all waiting for today. All of you of the War Memorial Commission have done a great job and Elvis and I are proud that we could play a small part in making the commission's dream come true."

The shrine was opened to the general public the following Wednesday, June 6, and since then, the *Arizona* Memorial has become one of the largest attractions on the island. But time and the elements took their toll on the memorial, and the wall needed replacement by the early 1980s. Under the leadership of National Commander Robert Martin of Louisiana, AMVETS was able to raise the funds needed to replace the old wall with a new sea-resistant one costing more than $50,000.

Construction began in December 1983 and was completed on Mar. 15, 1984. Stonecraft Memorial, Inc., of Honolulu, was responsible for the installa-

National Commander Robert Wilbraham and Auxiliary President Agnes Kolano address those gathered for the dedication of the new wall in 1984, with PNC Ralph Hall presiding as master of ceremonies.

tion of the new wall—a project to which Samuel K. Sasano, the company's president, and Bert Y. Morinaka, its vice president-manager, gave their personal attention. Morinaka continues his interest in the wall and is now owner and president of Stonecraft.

The Vermont Marble Company provided the special Imperial Danby white marble from its quarry in Danby, Vt., under contract with the AMVETS National Service Foundation.

The reconstructed memorial wall was rededicated on April 4, 1984. National Commander Robert L. Wilbraham of Mentor, Ohio, led a group which included Auxiliary President Agnes Kolano of LaPalma, Calif., and the president of National Service Foundation, Julius Pollatschek of Union, N.J., to place a wreath at the wall.

Past National Commander Ralph Hall of Summerland Keys, Fla., served as master of ceremonies as Gary Cummins, superintendent of the U.S.S. *Arizona* Memorial, accepted the gift on behalf of the American people. Welcoming remarks were offered by Maj. Gen. Alexis Lum, adjutant general of Hawaii, and Eileen

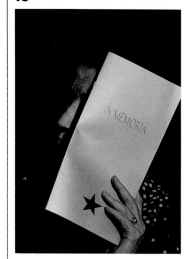

Anderson, mayor of the city and county of Honolulu. Jack Lord, star of the TV series "Hawaii Five-O," was on hand for the occasion as well. Lt. Gen. Charles G. Cooper, commanding general of Fleet Marine Force, Pacific, delivered the dedicatory address.

In December 1991, the AMVETS leadership traveled again to Pearl Harbor—this time to help commemorate the 50th anniversary of the bombing there. The delegation was led by National Commander James L. Singler of Sandusky, Ohio, who represented the organization at ceremonies aboard the *Arizona* on the morning of the 7th. He later laid an AMVETS wreath to the memory of those whose names are inscribed on the memorial wall and all others who had died during the war.

Following the ceremonies in Hawaii, AMVETS formally dedicated the *Arizona* Memorial Room at national headquarters in Lanham, Md., on December 15. Deputy Assistant Secretary of the Navy for Reserve Affairs Donald C. Morency keynoted the dedication, pointing out that "there is no more fitting organization to lead the way in this commemoration effort than you AMVETS." The room features the history of AMVETS' participation in the building of the wall, complete with a state-of-art audio presentation.

Over the years, AMVETS has continued its homage to the "Silent Crew" as each December 7 finds the group's national leadership at the Tomb of the Unknowns for a wreath laying. Similar honors are paid in Hawaii when AMVETS leaders visit the memorial as part of an annual fact-finding mission to the Far East each spring. AMVETS also provides Pearl Pins to veterans in hospitals—symbolic of an ongoing commitment to the veteran that began with World War II.

Most fitting of all, perhaps, will be the Silver Helmet Memorial Award given in 1994 to those 1,177 brave men. The 1,102 of them still entombed in the *Arizona*'s sunken hull gives simple, yet elegant, testimony to the price of freedom and the need for eternal vigilance.

—Danny Devine

After dedication of the Arizona Memorial Room at national headquarters, PNCs Wilbraham, Berc, Hall and Martin gather in the room with its designer, Tom Kozar.

This alarming revelation, however, carried with it a flip side or, as the committee described it, "our prescription for survival." Included were 29 proposals for reorganization. Among them was an increase in life memberships from $50 to $100 and an annual dues hike of $1 as well as cutbacks in departments and personnel.

The delegates approved the committee's recommendations and the overhaul got underway, culminating in a robust convention the following year addressed by President Kennedy, himself a former Massachusetts post commander. (The president, however, was not the only famous personage to have been an AMVET leader. Sen. Edmund S. Muskie from Maine had been national executive director [succeeding Elliott Newcomb] and Sen. Edward W. Brooke of Massachusetts, national judge advocate.)

Two months after Dante Spagnolo was elected national commander, the Cuban Missile Crisis erupted and AMVETS once more pledged its support to the commander-in-chief "to protect the cause of freedom." By 1963, AMVETS was again the "vigorous" organization it once had been. In November of that year, however, President Kennedy was assassinated. AMVETS had lost a true friend and it remained for National Commander Edmund M. Gulewicz to render final honors in a wreath-laying ceremony at the Kennedy gravesite on Dec. 7, 1963.

Two famous names in AMVETS history: John F. Kennedy and Edmund Muskie. On Pearl Harbor Day 1963, National Commander Edward Gulewicz and Auxiliary President Leah Monasterio place a wreath at the grave of the assassinated president.

Meanwhile, renewal in AMVETS took many forms. In the mid-sixties, Americanism received an added boost from what has become a long-standing relationship with Freedoms Foundation at Valley Forge. The AMVETS Auxiliary launched a nationwide fund-raising campaign in 1966 to assist the foundation. Since then, it has helped to fund various maintenance and improvement projects on the Valley Forge campus, has provided grants for teacher seminars and has even furnished several rooms in a foundation building.

A popular place to gather, whether for inspiration or renewal, Valley Forge was the site of a 1969 summit meeting involving the national commanders of the major veterans organizations. Joseph V. Ferrino represented AMVETS at the session attended by his counterparts from the DAV, the VFW and the American Legion.

In 1982, AMVETS joined with the foundation to erect a memorial carillon on the grounds and five years later—with the Auxiliary and the National Service Foundation—began sponsoring participation in the foundation's Youth Leadership Seminars. Winners of essay contests have their expenses paid (by the NSF) to the annual four-day conferences, where they participate in discussions with leaders from government, industry and the academic community as well as visit historic sites such as Ellis Island and Independence Hall.

On Dec. 10, 1969, AMVETS celebrated its 25th anniversary, with the nation's governors proclaiming a special week in honor of the occasion. Serving as national commander at the time was Robert B. Gomulinski, the first Korean War veteran to be elected to that post by a major veterans organization.

Attendees to the Freedoms Foundation Youth Leadership Seminar in 1989 pose against the skyline of New York during a visit to the Statue of Liberty.

As AMVETS moved into the 1970s under Robert W. Showalter, it once again became quite active in the formulation of national policy. The question of amnesty for deserters and "draft dodgers" of the Vietnam War is a case in point. National Commanders Joseph R. Sanson and Berge Avadanian went on record as strongly opposing any such pardon. Even so, by 1975, there was legislation before Congress that would have granted immunity to draft dodgers. Terming it "a shocking affront to veterans," National Commander Paul C. Welsh said at the time that "honorably serving the nation is something to be proud of and should not be soiled by legislation that would grant a hero's welcome to those who chose self above country." The measure, needless to say, was defeated.

While issues such as this occupied center stage in American politics, the daily business of operating an organization like AMVETS would grind on. And so would the group's financial needs. If anything, they continued to grow. Looking for ways to meet these needs, AMVETS under the leadership of Joseph F. Ramsey, Jr., opened its first thrift store on Georgia Avenue in Washington, D.C.

The nation was still celebrating its bicentennial four years later when Thomas J. McDonough became national commander. And by 1978, AMVETS was ready to move again. National Commander Frank D. Ruggiero and the National Executive Committee set the wheels in motion to sell the building on Rhode Island Avenue. Within two years' time, the organization had a new home—this time in Lanham, Md. Maryland Gov. Harry Hughes dedicated the building at 4647 Forbes Boulevard—appropriately enough on December 7, Pearl Harbor Day—during the term of Ernest F. Pitochelli.

From its new location, AMVETS continued to make its presence felt. In 1982, the organization under National Commander Donald R. Russell weighed in with strong support for President Reagan's "High Frontier," or anti-ballistic missile system in space.

Trucks of the National Service Foundation's thrift store operation pull double duty in community service, hauling emergency food and supplies to the needy in South Carolina after Hurricane Hugo swept through the state.

continued on page 50

New Home In Lanham

The concept (above) for the headquarters building moved a step closer to reality when on Dec. 1, 1979, National Commander Joseph Koralewski, VA Administrator Max Cleland (seated) and Lt. Gov. Samuel Bogley broke ground for the structure (right) at 4647 Forbes Boulevard. Among those pictured are Sen. Paul Sarbanes (behind Cleland) and Auxiliary President Lila Longworth.

At top, Earl Wright, building committee chairman, leads the Pledge of Allegiance on Dedication Day. Participating (from left) are National Chaplain Michael Filip, Auxiliary President Anne Brown, National Commander Ernest Pitochelli, and LaVerne McDonough, wife of the late Past National Commander Thomas McDonough. Above are the headquarters conference room and memorial chapel.

A Bust For LBJ

Housed in AMVETS National Headquarters, this bust of Lyndon B. Johnson, the 36th president of the United States, is one of four casts of a life-size bronze by sculptor Jimilu Mason of Alexandria, Va. The bust was Mr. Johnson's favorite portrait of himself. When he was Senate Majority Leader, he accurately predicted that the Washington Senators would defeat the Baltimore Orioles by a score of 9-2 in the game that opened the 1959 baseball season. His guess entitled him to that year's Lowell B. Mason Award, named for the former federal trade commissioner, a baseball fan and the artist's father. He elected to receive the bust as his reward.

Miss Mason sketched Johnson in his Senate office and later in the White House. Her work, in clay, was not cast in bronze until 1965. In addition to the bust shown here, the other casts are located at the National Portrait Gallery in Washington, The Johnson Space Center in Houston, and the Lyndon Baines Johnson Library and Museum in Austin, Tex.

continued from page 45

That same year, it initiated "Because We Care Day." Held the first Wednesday of April in VA medical centers across the country, this annual program lets hospitalized veterans know of "our concern for their well-being." In 1991 alone, some 15,000 personal care kits supplied by the National Service Foundation were distributed to patients by AMVETS volunteers. Working through the Veterans Affairs Voluntary Service (VAVS) program, these selfless men and women have contributed countless hours of their free time to working in the centers. Essley B. Burdine, national commander in 1974–75, performed, for example, more than 4,000 hours of voluntary service during his career.

Beyond the walls of these facilities, caring extended to another Wall—the Vietnam Veterans Memorial. Throughout the three–year battle for the memorial's authorization and design, AMVETS supplied vital congressional testimony and contributed close to $37,000 for its construction. Perhaps coincidental, but the organi-

Because We Care Day and support for the Wall were major initiatives. . .

zation was also the first veterans group to welcome Vietnam veterans as members. Under National Commander Lincoln S. Tamraz, AMVETS service officers had met returning Vietnam vets and offered them not only assistance but also free memberships. Finally, in 1987, James B. King would become the first Vietnam veteran to be elected national commander.

. . . And so was helping to restore the Statue of Liberty (left).

There was more, too. With John S. Lorec as national commander, AMVETS led the fight in 1985 to halt legislation that would have replaced veterans entitlements. A year later, it was participating in efforts to restore the Statue of Liberty. Under National Commander Robert A. Medairos, the organization contributed $100,000 of the more than $265 million needed for the restoration.

During this same period, AMVETS teamed up with the Disabled American Veterans, Paralyzed Veterans of America and the Veterans of Foreign Wars to produce the Independent Budget. The collaborative effort, undertaken when Joseph T. Piening was national commander, turned out to be unprecendeted. No pie-in-the-sky document, the IB each year has stood as an alternate to the VA budget the president submits. The figures it recommends are what the four groups have determined would adequately fund the department.

On Oct. 25, 1988, President Reagan signed Public Law 11–527, elevating VA to cabinet–level status as the Department of Veterans Affairs. It had been a long,

At Fort McNair in Washington, President Reagan signs the historic bill making VA a department as National Commander Jimmy Smith (second from right) looks on. Despite its lofty status, VA has continued to lack the funds needed to adequately care for the nation's veterans (above)—a situation reiterated each year in the Independent Budget.

uphill fight, starting eight years before when Joseph R. Koralewski was national commander. Jimmy T. Smith was now at the helm and America's veterans finally had a direct say–so in decisions affecting them and their families. "This bill does not give cabinet rank to just a government agency," affirmed the president. "It gives cabinet rank to every veteran." AMVETS and other veterans groups, which had pushed so hard for the legislation, had cause to celebrate.

But there was still work ahead. Within a year, President George Bush's war against illegal drugs was in full swing. "One of the keys to winning this fight is deepening the awareness of all Americans to the dangers of drug abuse." So wrote the president to National Commander Warren W. Eagles, Sr. AMVETS knew that some form of public education would be called for and had begun extensive research and development in the school districts of Grand Rapids, Mich., on a community education program called AMVETS Against Drug and Alcohol Abuse. Thanks to the efforts of Past National Commander Ted Leszkiewicz, A.A.D.A.A. (pronounced *aid–dah*) has grown from one participating state to thirteen, while attracting White House and congressional attention.

Such mobilization was readily apparent in 1992, when a so-called rural health care initiative by the federal government threatened veterans benefits. The secretaries of veterans affairs and health and human services had proposed opening the doors of two selected VA medical centers (Salem, Va., and Tuskegee, Ala.) to treatment of non–veterans.

AMVETS, under National Commander James L. Singler, immediately voiced opposition to the move and vowed to continue to oppose it "as long as there is one honorably separated veteran who goes without proper health care." Other veterans organizations also denounced it as letter–writing campaigns directed at the White House and Capitol Hill were mounted. So great was the outcry from the veterans community that the proposal was soon dropped.

The decade of the nineties has also seen AMVETS in the forefront of such issues as increasing unemployment compensation for ex–service members; maintaining

Available through the National Service Foundation, thousands of AMVETS Desert Shield and Desert Storm flags flew in support of U.S. troops serving in the Persian Gulf, who later came home to rousing victory parades in New York and Washington (right).

the integrity of the VA rating schedule; and eliminating the waiver of retired pay by veterans receiving service–connected disability compensation. It has also maintained a continual vigil on the question of America's POW/MIAs and, under Vaughn L. Brown, Sr., marched astride the Bush administration in support of Operation *Desert Storm* during the Persian Gulf War.

As the organization approaches the 21st century, much still remains to be done. Having already pledged its support for President Bill Clinton's plan to rebuild America by abandoning the "something for nothing" ethic, AMVETS continues to be ever vigilant that veterans and their families are served fairly. "We have purchased the right, often with shattered bodies and minds, to be empowered and offered expanded choices," stressed National Commander James J. Kenney.

The significance of that statement has not been lost on the current administration. For AMVETS today continues to be a key player under National Commander Donald M. Hearon in the public policy arena on such issues as MIA accountability and VA health care reform.

What does the future hold for AMVETS? The answer may very well lie in the words of one of its early leaders. "As I look down the path of our future," said Harold A. Keats, 1948–49 national commander, "I envision a mature AMVET organization, well–equipped and girded for battle, continuing the fight on the home-front for the perpetuation of the American way of life as we did in uniform on the battlefields of the world." If the first half–century of AMVETS service is any indication, this nation's veterans are in good hands.

—Dick Flanagan and Patrick McCaffrey

With the leaders of other veterans groups, National Commander Donald Hearon (near door) *participates in a POW/MIA meeting at the White House with President Clinton, Secretary of State Warren Christopher* (right of president) *and administration officials.*

Voices

From the White House

It is a source of great satisfaction a
reassurance to know that those of
you who achieved victory in Worl
War II are working for a strong and
unified America.

—HARRY S. TRUM

Your members are a vital part of
America's strength. And your
unselfish efforts, both in war and
peace, fortify our society and the
traditions on which it was founded.

—RICHARD M. NIXON

Your civilian patriotic activities have
sustained and strengthened the principles for which you fought. And
your efforts have made your communities better places in which to live.

—GERALD R. FORD

AMVETS has played an important
role in advocating and supporting
programs assisting veterans and
in aiding those charged with . . .
administering these programs.

—JIMMY CART

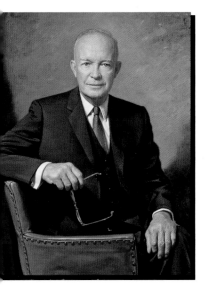

*ur organization's support of efforts
strengthen our nation's security
s helped lessen the danger of
gressive war by those who fear
d hate freedom.*

—DWIGHT D. EISENHOWER

*You have continually shown that
you are willing and capable of exert-
ing the kind of responsible leadership which is an honor to you and
an inspiration to others.*

—JOHN F. KENNEDY

*Your sacrifices, in both war and
peace, helped pave the way toward
a goal that is still very much with us
today—a world of freedom and of
opportunity for every human being.*

—LYNDON B. JOHNSON

*ur wonderful record of service to
terans and their families pays fit-
g homage to our heroes and to the
als for which they answered the
l to arms.*

—RONALD REAGAN

*The members of your organization
have not only helped fellow veterans
to make the transition back into civilian life but also set an example of
enduring patriotism and concern. . . .*

—GEORGE BUSH

*You can take pride in your contribu-
tion to the American legacy of service to our fellow citizens. I com-
mend you for your deep concern for
those who . . . sacrifice for freedom.*

—BILL CLINTON

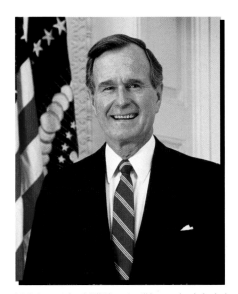

Through The Years
1944/1955

From top left, National Commander Edgar Corry visits Shick General Hospital in Illinois; an early AMVETS convention gets in full swing; Auxiliary members comfort a hospitalized veteran; Joe Palooka, comic strip heavyweight champion during the 1940s and 1950s, signed on as an AMVETS member over a nationwide radio broadcast.

A photographic retrospective of people, places and events over the past 50 years in AMVETS

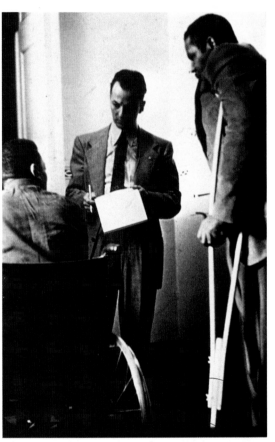

From top right, President Harry Truman (inset) dedicates the headquarters on Rhode Island Avenue, then wraps up a tour of the building with National Commander John Smith; National Commander Henry Mahady addresses a convention; President Dwight Eisenhower and "Little Miss AMVET"; Sad Sacks hijinks; a service officer on the job.

Through The Years
1956/1969

AMVETS
AMERICAN
BOOKSHELF

Presented to free peoples, that they may understand the American Way of Life

The Art of Teaching

*From top right, National Commander A. Leo Anderson aboard the U.S.S. Franklin D. Roosevelt in Tonkin Bay; National Auxiliary President June Miller presents an AMVETS bookshelf to Korean Ambassador You Chan Yang; National Commander Winston Burdine (dark suit, center) prepares to fly to Russia; National Commander Joseph Ferrino at Valley Forge VSO summit; National Commander Dante Spagnolo and Auxiliary President Alice Oana view an AMVETS sports kit; Medal of Honor recipient Audie Murphy becomes a member; Film star Marilyn Monroe promotes the White Clover Program.**

*The White Clover, meaning "Remember Me," is the official flower of AMVETS. Found not only in America but around the world, it symbolizes the states from which U.S. Armed Forces were drawn and the worldwide battlefields on which they fought.

From top right, National Commander Lincoln Tamraz burns the paid headquarters mortgage; below he is joined by House Veterans' Affairs Committee Chairman Olin Teague (front, second from right) and six past and future national commanders at ground-breaking ceremonies in 1965 (can you spot them?). World War II ace Pappy Boyington tries on his hat as a new member of California Post 56.

Through The Years
1970/1983

From top right, Jerry Dubord, a Junior AMVETS leader in Escanaba, Mich., delivers a speech on Americanism; elsewhere, in California, AMVETS awards another ROTC medal; PNC Essley Burdine and Donald Russell at the latter's installation as national commander; an audiologist works with a youngster at the John Tracy Clinic; Pope Paul VI greets National Commander Robert Gomulinski, who presented the pontiff with the Silver Helmet Peace Award, National Commander Ted Leszkiewicz poses with a March of Dimes poster child.

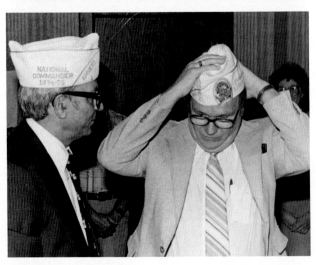

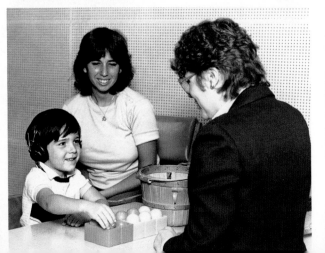

From top left, National Commander Joseph Koralewski has a word with House Veterans' Affairs Committee Chairman Ray Roberts; a youngster on an AMVETS-sponsored T-ball team takes his cuts; National Commander Robert Showalter inspects M-16s at the Colt Firearms Company; National Commander Joseph Sanson (left) shakes hands with Department of New Jersey Judge Advocate Lester Garo after testifying before Congress; National Commander Frank Ruggiero and members of the national headquarters staff.

Through The Years
1984/1994

From top right, an Oklahoma AMVET tends to an elderly patient; National Commander John Lorec lines up with members of New York Post 18; National Commander James King, accompanied by National Executive Director Morgan Ruph, testifies before Congress; National Commander Vaughn Brown and VACRS Chairman Hsu Li-nung sign a brotherhood proclamation at the 1991 national convention in Louisville; an AMVET dressed as Santa spreads some Christmas cheer.

From top left, National Commander Joseph Piening congratulates a Special Olympics winner; National Commander Donald Hearon and Auxiliary President Barbara Hinsley, together with Pearl Harbor survivor Tony DiLorenza, lay a wreath at Arlington Cemetery on Pearl Harbor Day; DESERT STORM veterans in California and a message that says it all; PNC Joe Ramsey presents the Silver Helmet Americanism Award to Richard Michel of Buffalo; thanks to the efforts of Post 920, the largest flying U.S. flag in the country waves proudly at Gastonia, N.C.

Badge
of
Office

*A closer look at the stars worn
by national commanders
reveals some subtle
distinctions in styling*

Elmo Keel *1945*
Jack Hardy *1946*
Ray Sawyer *1947*
Edward C. Corry, Jr. *1948*
Harold A. Keats *1949*
Harold S. Russell *1950-51*
John L. Smith *1952*
Marshall E. Miller *1953*
Henry J. Mahady *1954*
Rufus H. Wilson *1955*
Rudolph G. Pesata *1956*

Joseph R. Sanson *1973*
Berge Avadanian *1974*
Essley B. Burdine *1975*
Paul C. Welsh *1976*
Thomas J. McDonough *1977*
Frank D. Ruggiero *1978*
Ted Leszkiewicz *1979*
Joseph R. Koralewski *1980*

Ralph E. Hall *1966*
A. Leo Anderson *1967*
Anthony J. Caserta *1968*
Joseph V. Ferrino *1969*
Robert B. Gomulinski *1970*
Robert W. Showalter *1971*
Joe F. Ramsey, Jr. *1972*

Dominick L. Strada *1957*
Stuart J. Satullo *1958*
Winston E. Burdine *1959*
Harold T. Berc *1960*
Harold S. Russell *1961*
Edwin P. Fifielski *1962*
Dante E. Spagnolo *1963*
Edmund M. Gulewicz *1964*
Lincoln S. Tamraz *1965*

Ernest F. Pitochelli *1981*
Donald R. Russell *1982*
Robert Martin *1983*
Robert L. Wilbraham *1984*
John S. Lorec *1985*
Robert A. Medairos *1986*
Joseph T. Piening *1987*
James B. King *1988*
Jimmy T. Smith *1989*
Warren W. Eagles, Sr. *1990*
Vaughn L. Brown, Sr. *1991*
James L. Singler *1992*
James J. Kenney *1993*

Donald M. Hearon *1994*

*Recalling the founding
and development of
AMVETS and its auxiliary*

Albert C. Geremia. Approximately 70 men were present at that meeting in Kansas City, but I didn't count them. After establishing the purposes of the organization, we went on to the constitution and bylaws. Needless to say, all of this was accomplished after much discussion and debate. We knew we would eventually encounter many organizational headaches. Even so, we knew we had to draw up a program that would appeal to all veterans of World War II.

We then set forth objectives for the future growth of AMVETS. In a group of 70 veterans, there was no lack of ideas on how we should proceed. One thing for sure, we knew we had some important goals that required immediate attention.

Membership was the first goal. To accomplish this, we had to have the financial resources and we had to get the word out to millions of veterans that we had established an organization they could relate to when they returned to civilian life.

Next came publicity. We knew full well that in order to get this message out to all veterans of WWII, we needed publicity and this was not easy to come by, especially at that time. We were competing with the Manhattan Project, Sen. Joe McCarthy and his hearings, and the illness of President Roosevelt.

We then set out to establish a national headquarters in Washington, D.C. We had elected Elmo Keel from Washington as national commander; Carl Freudenberg from Ohio as finance officer; T. Paul Moody from Los Angeles as judge advocate; Claude Morgan, also from Los Angeles, as public relations officer; and myself as national executive director. Gen. Horacio Holdridge was selected as an advisor.

Soon after we settled in on M Street, Eleanor Roosevelt invited us to the White House for a dinner meeting to discuss AMVETS and its goals. Upon the group's arrival at the White House, she ushered us into the East Room for the meal, while Secret Service agents posted themselves at various points around the room.

After some small talk, Mrs. Roosevelt asked, "Why AMVETS?" I responded, "For the perpetuation of world peace." She then wanted to know how we planned to carry this out. I told her we had an idea that veterans from all over the world would one day meet as a body to determine world affairs. After all, they were the ones who had the hands-on experience with war and knew the value of human life.

Dinner concluded about 9 p.m. While Ruth Purcell, a close friend of Mrs. Roosevelt's, took the others on a tour of the White House, Mrs. Roosevelt took me into the Lincoln Room and invited me to sit at Lincoln's desk and to hold the pen he used to write the Gettysburg Address. Needless to say, I was dumbfounded.

As we were leaving the White House, Miss Purcell grabbed me and said that Mrs. Roosevelt liked the way AMVETS was headed and would give us all the support she possibly could. The story of that meeting was carried by *Army Times, Stars and Stripes* and major newspapers across the country. As a result, we began to receive letters from veterans wanting to know how they could join AMVETS.

Our next big break came during the first national convention in Chicago. Stan Allen, who had become public relations officer, introduced me to John F. Kennedy, a congressman from Massachusetts. Kennedy invited me into the lobby to sit down, because his back was bothering him. We began talking and he sprang the question, Why AMVETS? I proceeded to tell him what we were about.

Kennedy struck me as being a highly intelligent young man with a lot of character and integrity. Some of the ideas we talked about that evening were actually laced into his inaugural address. I was really excited about this when Kennedy became a candidate for president, because I remembered our discussion in Chicago—and how he would be such a great help to AMVETS.

With publicity finally taking root, our next objective was a congressional charter.

continued on page 84

Reflections

Reflections

AUG. 10, 1914–JAN. 15, 1969

Elmo W. Keel. In addition to being one of the 18 founders of AMVETS, Elmo Keel served as its first national commander. He will always be remembered by the organization and its members for the devotion that he bestowed on the infant organization in its first days and which continued until his death.

—AMVETS 25th Anniversary Book

APR. 27, 1904–JULY 3, 1955

Jack W. Hardy. Jack Hardy continued the work of making the young organization into one that would be accepted by all. He instituted THE NATIONAL AMVET publication. His job was to recruit the returning veterans of World War II, since most began streaming home during his term. His tremendous organizing skill imprinted its mark on AMVETS and has stood it in good stead these 25 years.

—AMVETS 25th Anniversary Book

Ray Sawyer. Ray Sawyer presided over the organization when AMVETS received its congressional charter. The membership of the organization doubled during his term. He also began many of the programs that still are part of the organization.

—AMVETS 25th Anniversary Book

MAR. 25, 1912–OCT. 9, 1968

Edgar C. Corry, Jr. His term was one of progress. The membership kept increasing. The organization moved into larger quarters in Washington. He established National Preparedness Day on Apr. 18, 1948, and the whole nation observed it with AMVETS. *—AMVETS 25th Anniversary Book*

National Commanders

Harold A. Keats. The year I held office may have been the apex of the public relations effort. Under the direction of Stan Allen, a Neiman Scholarship graduate of Yale University and a professional newsman, I was able to enhance my personal association with top officials like President Harry S. Truman.

That year began on a rough note. The first week in office, I was informed that there was not enough money in the bank for payroll, so I borrowed $10,000 from the bank. But, there were many bright spots in my term as the year quickly moved along. The first direct mail fundraising was implemented; the scholarship program began to operate and the national service foundation was organized.

Soon-to-be President John Kennedy was appointed housing chairman, and Dean Rusk, who became secretary of state, chaired the International Affairs Committee. Ed Muskie, who went on to be governor, senator, secretary of state and a presidential candidate, became AMVETS national executive director. Many of the nation's leaders—including President Truman, Gen. George C. Marshall, Admiral [Paul] Nimitz—personally accepted life memberships in AMVETS from myself.

Among the programs sponsored by AMVETS back then was the Delta Bowl and teenage basketball. The latter project was designed to go on forever, like American Legion baseball, but someone dropped the ball.

In 1949, we had the president of the United States at our national convention in Iowa—the only AMVETS convention ever to be so honored—and installed the first carillon at Arlington National Cemetery.

Harold S. Russell. Harold Russell was the only AMVET to hold the office of national commander more than once. He was re-elected in 1950 for his second term. This famous worldwide personality, who personified what a disabled veteran was capable of, gave AMVETS inspiration during his three terms, but he also gave [the organization] leadership. *—AMVETS 25th Anniversary Book*

John L. Smith. His administration was highlighted by the purchase and dedication of the first owned national headquarters, which was the site of the present national headquarters. During his term, AMVETS became part of the World Veterans Federation. Membership also increased under this dynamic man. *—AMVETS 25th Anniversary Book*

AUG. 27, 1913–OCT. 7, 1958

Marshall E. Miller. Commander Miller made great strides in the area of leading AMVETS into more international cooperation with the World Veterans Federation and he worked hard for more AMVET participation in the affairs of the United Nations.
—AMVETS 25th Anniversary Book

JULY 1, 1916–SEPT. 12, 1989

Henry J. Mahady. During Commander Mahady's term of office, AMVETS' prestige as a service organization grew. In 1954, our scholarship winners received national attention from presentations by President Eisenhower and Vice President Nixon, plus TV coverage on the "Today Show" and other prominent TV and radio programs.
—AMVETS 25th Anniversary Book

Rufus H. Wilson. This popular national commander began his service with AMVETS as a service officer and eventually became its national service director. He served as commander during the 10th anniversary of our organization. He worked hard at keeping AMVETS the top service organization that it has become. He also made the first presentation of a Silver Helmet Award and it was to Gen. George C. Marshall.
—AMVETS 25th Anniversary Book

SEPT. 11, 1914–DEC. 12, 1964

Rudolph G. Pesata. Rudy Pesata was a real "grassroots" AMVET who always served his organization well, whether he was a member of a post or the national commander. During his term, he pushed for an even greater community effort by AMVET posts to go along with the fine service program of the organization. He felt that the community deserved as much time as individual AMVETS could offer.
—AMVETS 25th Anniversary Book

National Commanders

Dominick L. Strada. He was elected national commander in one of the closest elections in AMVET history, proving that AMVETS is and has always been an authentic "grassroots" organization. Commander Strada inaugurated the "Gold Brick Drive," which was intended to clear up the debt on the national headquarters [mortgage].
—AMVETS 25th Anniversary Book

OCT. 27, 1904–NOV. 3, 1982

Stuart J. Satullo. Only a few days after beginning my term in office as national commander, the Russians launched their earth satellite Sputnik I. This action seemed to set the stage for the coming year. The print and broadcast media reports in the wake of the Sputnik announcement indicated that civilians were panicky and confused. At the time, I was a guest of Secretary of Defense [Charles] Wilson and was visiting military installations. The military men were much calmer than the civilian population. There was concern, yes, but there also was confidence.

In 1957 AMVETS maintained its active role in the World Veterans Federation Conference held in West Berlin, representing more than 20 million veterans from 135 veterans groups in 35 countries. During the Berlin W.V.F. conference, I presented an AMVETS American Bookshelf to James Owusas, president of the Ghana Veterans Group. AMVETS also played a major role in ceremonies at the Capitol Rotunda on May 30, 1958. After I presented the Silver Helmet to the Unknown Soldiers of World War II and the Korean conflict, they were laid to rest alongside the Unknown Soldier of World War I at Arlington Cemetery.

At the annual Cook County AMVETS Banquet at the Morrison Hotel in Chicago, I called for the elimination of the Joint Chiefs of Staff to reduce unnecessary duplication in and by the armed services. When the program ended, I was handed a telegram endorsing my plan. It read, "I have just learned of your vigorous statement in behalf of the Defense Reorganization Plan. My congratulations on your call for action. You and AMVETS have my deep appreciation for this unqualified support on the issue of security and solvency which has been joined in Congress. Signed, Dwight D. Eisenhower."

Later in my term, I called on Congress to free some $800 million in World War II enemy assets, which was invested at 2-1/4 percent interest, and suggested the money could be used for G.I. home loans at 4 percent interest. But the primary theme of my year was "Progressive Americanism," which stressed the good things of the nation while focusing on the benefits accruing to all Americans.

Winston E. Burdine, M.D. "Doc" Burdine was a traveling representative of AMVETS, both in the United States and [around] the world. He traveled to Russia to visit the World War II battlegrounds of Russia under the auspices of the People to People Program. He represented us well in the World Veterans Federation. He was a strong and forceful leader. This leadership was recognized when the 12th AMVETS carillon was dedicated on May 30, 1968, at the U.S. National Cemetery at Marietta, Ga.
—AMVETS 25th Anniversary Book

FEB. 20, 1914–JAN. 7, 1967

Reflections

Harold T. Berc. Without question, the chief achievement of my term was AMVETS' involvement with the U.S.S. *Arizona* Memorial. Our first effort consisted of installing a carillon aboard the U.S.S. *Arizona.* We were able to raise the funds necessary to inscribe the names of the lost 1,102 members of her crew on a memorial wall. In dedicating the carillon, I found that the Pacific War Memorial Commission was short $200,000 in 1959 for funding the memorial. This set me off. I pointed out to the public that if each crewmen were interred separately, he would have automatically received a $250 burial allowance from the Veteran's Administration.

President Eisenhower had announced that he would veto any appropriation that could not be classified as an emergency. This position chilled all efforts to get congressional aid. In a meeting with Ike, I pointed out the gross injustice of the involuntary burial of 1,102 crewmen in the hull of the *Arizona*. Ike not only agreed that a congressional appropriation of the amount needed would not be vetoed, but he authorized me to herald his position. The rest, as they say, is history.

I have always believed that AMVETS should recognize women and minority veterans as well as the belief in God. So, to capture membership on a national basis, the Women's Post-at-Large was created and publicized as well as the Four Chaplain's Memorial Post. I also sought to broaden our vision with a strong brotherhood program. An attractive plaque featuring the Four Chaplains aboard the *Dorchester* was given at the national convention to every post that had established one meaningful brotherhood program.

Another idea I implemented concerned the smaller AMVET posts. On occasion, these posts wished the national commander would make an appearance at various functions. So I offered to tape an invigorating speech geared to their special affairs. I also made 1,000 records of a vigorous rallying speech on membership and sent them out to all posts. I noticed that small posts often struggled with communications by way of one-page mimeographed newsletters. I encouraged every post to send their paper to me for review and comment. This led to the creation of the first publications contest.

During my term, I also urged that national conventions have a special objective. I started with my convention and made its theme "Our National Purpose." It was a beautifully ordered event, highlighted by live telephone speeches by both presidential candidates—Jack Kennedy and Dick Nixon. Another important event of my outgoing convention was a beautiful memorial program that highlighted the brotherhood theme in a pageant written and produced by my late wife Mary. Lastly, to preserve the history of AMVETS up to 1960, I arranged for the production of a slide history, which I have narrated.

Edwin P. Fifielski. Commander Fifielski made civil defense his major program during his term of office. The AMVET Civil Defense Caravan traveled 45,000 miles through 37 states. The caravan had as its feature a model fallout shelter.

—AMVETS 25th Anniversary Book

OCT. 4, 1916–JUNE 2, 1985

National Commanders

Dante E. Spagnolo. My year as national commander was rewarding to me, both in the wealth of experience I gained and in the wealth of friends I made. It was filled with deep, personal satisfaction.

I participated in numerous events, such as serving as honorary grand marshal in the 1962 Veterans Day Parade in San Francisco, Calif., and was proud to be a part of the firm support AMVETS gave to President John F. Kennedy during the Cuban Crisis to protect the cause of freedom.

AMVETS continued to take action on other key issues. On Jan. 13, 1963, I sent a telegram to Richard Cardinal Cushing, archbishop of Boston, offering to work with him to bring about the speedy release of American prisoners held in Cuba. In a similar telegram, I asked Fidel Castro for permission to visit Cuba and discuss the release of American prisoners. Then, in May of that year, I visited East and West Berlin as a part of the 10th General Assembly of the World Veterans Federation held in Copenhagen, Denmark, and had an audience with the Pope at the Vatican.

Soon after, I paid a visit to President Kennedy. The highlight of the meeting was the announcement and presentation of a $2,000 scholarship, in his name, to students who desired to specialize in teaching mentally retarded children.

The honors I received in your name mean so much to me and have been so personally gratifying. None of it, of course, would have been possible without the suggestions, assistance, cooperation and hard work of so many individuals—among them National Auxiliary President Alice Oana.

Edmund M. Gulewicz. Many AMVETS programs continued to be carried out during the term of Edmund Gulewicz of Detroit, Mich. He was national commander at the time of the death of President John Kennedy and placed a wreath at the Kennedy grave on Dec. 7, 1963. His year . . . was highlighted at the 1964 convention in Philadelphia when Secretary of State Dean Rusk was the banquet speaker.

—AMVETS 25th Anniversary Book

MAR. 29, 1915–AUG. 12, 1991

Lincoln S. Tamraz. I am proud and honored to state that we, the officers and membership on all levels of AMVETS, had a productive and rewarding year.

We strengthened, for example, our relationship with the Department of Defense that resulted in special trips for the NEC, such as to Cape Canaveral and Germany.

I had the honor of representing President Lyndon B. Johnson on several occasions at various veterans activities. I also laid the groundwork for the dedication of our new headquarters on Rhode Island Avenue by President Johnson. At this time, I established the President Lyndon B. Johnson Scholarship Award and presented the president with a special Silver Helmet.

Within my term of office, there were two special projects I helped implement. In the first project, I worked with national service foundation lawyers and accountants for two years to reduce a proposed $2,000,000 IRS bill to less than $100,000. In the second project, I visited the "Garden of Patriots" in Florida and convinced "Golf American" to pay for and install a carillon in the garden. Soon after, I helped secure Bob Hope as master of ceremonies for the dedication.

Other highlights of my term were my address to both the House and the Senate; participation with Freedoms Foundation; visits to the FBI Academy, the Strategic Air

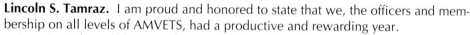

Command in Nebraska, Guantanimo Bay, Vandenburg Air Force Base; and the organization of five posts.

I secured funding from the national service foundation for the AMVET memorial carillon at Freedoms Foundation and raised funds for the drum and bugle corps in Randolph, Mass. As national commander, I also served on the Inaugural Committee in 1964 and chaired the AMVET delegation to the World Veterans Federation in Europe. There were many other highlights—one of which was very special. I was able to burn the national headquarters mortgage as the outgoing commander at the national convention in Boston, Mass.

Ralph E. Hall. With the formation of the John F. Kennedy Memorial Post No. 109 in Washington, D.C., AMVETS had the unique distinction, at that time, of being the only nationally chartered veterans organization where every member of Congress who served in the Armed Forces held a life membership.

As national commander, I had the pleasure of being present for the signing of the Cold War G.I. Bill by President Lyndon B. Johnson on Mar. 3, 1966. Afterwards, I received one of the pens used in signing the bill. When H.R. 13284 was introduced by Congressman Peter Rodino of New Jersey to open membership rolls to Vietnam veterans, it would be a highlight of any national commander's term.

I also participated in the Cape Coral carillon dedication with comedian Bob Hope, Connie Mack, Jr., and Miss U.S.A. Diana Batts. But there is one dedication that will always hold a special memory—the July 23, 1966, dedication of the national headquarters on Rhode Island Avenue. I was fortunate to be able to preside over that dedication in which President Johnson was the principal speaker. This was, indeed, the highlight of my tenure as national commander.

A. Leo Anderson. A very fine program for youth was initiated during Commander Anderson's administration. It was Operation Driver Excellence, which was a program where 75,000 young people from all over the country participated. The program was held in conjunction with the Dodge Car and Truck Division of Chrysler Motors. The finals were held at Soldiers Field in Chicago.

—*AMVETS 25th Anniversary Book*

MAR. 12, 1918–DEC. 7, 1974

Anthony J. Caserta. Commander Caserta has long been a vital cog in the AMVET wheel. He had been president of the national service foundation before being elected national commander at Hollywood, Fla., in August 1967. During his term of office, the United States was in constant turmoil with war in Vietnam and domestic problems. His constant theme was "Freedom by Positive Action."

—*AMVETS 25th Anniversary Book*

National Commanders

Joseph V. Ferrino. Commander Ferrino made the words "A Time for Re-Assessment" his theme for his term. He set his goal to increase membership and the efficiency of the organization. His program for cooperating with President Nixon in reducing tensions received wide attention from the . . . communication media. He represented AMVETS at the Apollo 8 launching and at St. Lo in France . . . as the guest of the French Government [for] the 25th anniversary of D-Day. His three major aims for the year were to [recognize] law enforcement officers with the theme of "Law and Order"; [reaffirm] AMVETS commitment to the Scouting Program; and [encourage] AMVET posts to sponsor and continue to sponsor Boy Scout troops . . . he continued liaison with national, state and local leaders in [the field] of legislation.

—AMVETS 25th Anniversary Book

Robert B. Gomulinski. "I pledge to you my untiring efforts to ensure AMVETS a year of growth in a year which I pray we shall see peace in Vietnam and the return of the major portion of our American troops from Southeast Asia." With these words, Bob Gomulinski began his term as the first Korean War veteran to head a major veterans organization and the youngest national commander of AMVETS.

His term was a memorable one from the start. It was the 25th anniversary of AMVETS and the governors proclaimed the week of Dec. 6-13, 1969, as "AMVETS 25th Anniversary Week." Bob later urged cities to sponsor patriotic and Americanism programs, and he called for additional federal funding to train more doctors.

On Apr. 28, 1970, he presented the AMVETS Gold Helmet Award to President Richard Nixon at the White House. Four months later, he led an AMVET delegation to Pope Paul VI's summer home at Castlegondolfo, Italy, where His Holiness was presented with the AMVETS Silver Helmet Peace Award.

On May 15, 1991, in Seoul, Korea, Bob was posthumously honored with the Korean Veterans Association's Ambassador of Peace Award. *—PNC Dante Spagnolo*

DEC. 10, 1931–DEC. 4, 1989

Robert W. Showalter. I am pleased with the organization as it has been a year of progress. I am grateful to those who worked so diligently in the realm of membership, as we are enjoying the most successful year in our history . . . . My greatest personal reward was that of your friendship, as I have traveled this great nation of ours meeting new friends—and I have found a common bond between all, a compassion to assist all mankind, and that truly has made me a better person.

—NEC Report, 27th National Convention

Joe F. Ramsey, Jr. At the AMVETS National Convention in Los Angeles in August 1971, I was the first national commander elected from the state of Texas and the first to assume leadership on September 1; previously, it was October 1.

My year as national commander was marked with the second largest increase in membership ever—a record that still stands more than 20 years later. I am doubly proud of this membership increase because it occurred in a year plagued with financial problems.

I could not participate in any trips outside the contiguous United States because of the lack of funds, and my travel to posts and installations within our borders was often supplemented by the local group being visited.

At the time Bob Gomulinski assumed the position of national executive director from PNC Ralph Hall, who had joined the Department of Labor, we conducted a survey of the national service foundation, then located in Alliance, Ohio, to ascertain the possibility of financial assistance to help the national headquarters meet various program requirements. The survey concluded that there were not adequate funds to assist the headquarters to carry on these vital programs.

Looking for ways to supplement our income, I asked Kenneth Cain to come to Washington and his trip resulted in the establishment of the first AMVETS Thrift Store on Georgia Avenue in Washington, D.C. Over the years, our thrift stores have helped us meet our growing financial needs.

Since my travel funds were meager, I spend much of my time in legislative efforts, where my background as an attorney, experience in veterans affairs, and political activity in Texas stood me in good stead on Capitol Hill.

As my term as national commander drew to a close, I was offered a position as judge on the Naval Court of Appeals by the secretary of the navy. At the same time, it was imperative to fill the position of executive director of the national service foundation and move those facilities from Ohio to national headquarters in Washington, D.C. A search was conducted to fill the executive director position and when no suitable candidate was found, I was asked to temporarily fill the position at the end of my term and assume the task of relocating the foundation.

At the end of a year, the Navy requested that I assume the judge's position or release it to be filled by someone else. Meanwhile, we had not found anyone willing to be executive director of a failing service foundation on the brink of bankruptcy. My love for AMVETS left me no choice; I released the position with the Navy and remained as executive director of the national service foundation. Since that day, I pledged to AMVETS that my efforts would assure that no future commander would serve under the dire financial circumstances that engulfed my year.

Joseph R. Sanson. With the cessation of hostilities in Vietnam, we must be prepared to render maximum assistance to our returning servicemen. I have assigned this as a matter of . . . [top] priority. . . . I know you share my feelings that we must stand ready, at all levels of AMVETS, to put forth every effort to assure these brave young men that their sacrifices shall not be forgotten. Needless to say, we will continue as always to provide service and counseling to World War II and Korean War veterans.

—THE NATIONAL AMVET

JUNE 15, 1911–OCT. 28, 1989

Berge Avadanian. When I became national commander, it was during a period of turmoil both in our country and in AMVETS. The Vietnam conflict had just ended and the bitterness and sadness after that bloody catastrophe lingered. The lukewarm acceptance by Americans, and even by our government, of returning servicemen was a source of resentment to those unsung heroes who sacrificed so much in a doubtful cause. The disgrace of the Watergate scandal, the public trials, revelations and convictions of government officials would further disillusion people.

Our organization at the time was trying to recover from deep financial problems resulting from mismanagement and a sharp reduction of income into the AMVETS National Service Foundation, our major source of funds for service programs. The public antagonism toward veterans and the military because of Vietnam resulted in a dismal response to our fund-raising appeals. The service foundation was faced with IRS audits and our whole financial structure was in danger.

AMVETS began to reverse the downward financial spiral when the mailing operations of the foundation were transferred from Ohio to national headquarters in Washington under the management of PNC Joe F. Ramsey, Jr. As commander, I maintained the national organization on the smallest budget in years and absorbed one-third of the national service department's costs, without borrowing funds.

While in office, I was invited to the White House on different occasions for formal functions, meetings and wide-ranging consultations. There were also meetings with every member of the president's cabinet on a range of mutual concerns.

I also was able to spearhead the reestablishment of the Organization of National Commanders of Major Veterans Groups and, in 1973, led a delegation to Paris for a meeting of the World Veterans Federation. After this, I traveled to Rome for a meeting with Ambassador [John] Volpe, and an audience with Pope Paul VI.

Following the torture and imprisonment of Israeli soldiers during the Yom Kippur War, my strong condemnation of the Syrians regarding these atrocities appeared in the press. As a result, I was invited by Prime Minister Golda Mier, together with other veteran leaders, to inspect battlefields and veterans hospitals in Israel.

In 1974, I made three Radio Free Asia broadcasts beamed to Southeast Asia, pleading for the release and accounting of missing Americans. On behalf of AMVETS, I voiced strong opposition to granting amnesty for deserters and draft dodgers to Presidents Nixon and Ford, members of Congress and the public.

By the end of my term of office, AMVETS membership had increased, the net worth of the organization had improved and the indebtedness of the national department had dramatically been reduced.

Essley B. Burdine. PNC Essley Burdine . . . contributed as much as anyone to making AMVETS the type of veterans organization we all can be proud of . . . . Mr. Burdine was in the Army Signal Corps in World War II. He joined AMVETS June 24, 1963 and was a life member of Georgia Post 1. —*THE NATIONAL AMVET*

OCT. 13, 1922–JAN. 22, 1991

Paul C. Welsh. After 2-1/2 years of intense campaigning against two very formidable opponents, I was elected on the second ballot, thanks to Thomas McDonough who was elected commander the following year.

Toni Gomulinski was elected national president at the auxiliary convention. We shared a most congenial, friendly and productive year, touring most departments and posts accompanied by my wife Betty and Toni's husband, PNC Robert Gomulinski, both now deceased.

During my term, AMVETS was in charge of the Veterans Day ceremonies at Arlington National Cemetery and I had the honor of escorting President Gerald R. Ford to the Tomb of the Unknowns as he placed the presidential wreath. Later in the morning, I placed the AMVETS wreath at the tomb.

Another highlight was an interesting and educational trip to Korea, sponsored by the Korean Veterans Association. There, I had the honor of addressing 3,000 Korean veterans on the 20th anniversary of the end of the Korean War.

One very amusing incident occurred in Texas when Toni and I were asked to mount horses for photographs—even though Toni had never been on a horse and did not desire to do so. It took more than 30 minutes to assure her that it was safe and being a good sport, she got on the horse. But I can still see the fear in her eyes for a few seconds before she started smiling.

Bobby Gujral was hired during my term in office and was a great asset to the national department, and continues to be for the foundation. Bobby, Joe Ramsey and Elias Lambrakopoulos [the national printer] are the only employees still at the headquarters today that were there in 1975-76.

My outgoing convention was held in Philadelphia, Pa. We received more media coverage at this convention than ever because of the discovery of Legionnaires' disease in the area a few weeks prior. It took a lot of soul-searching and many, many telephone conversations with health organizations, city and state officials before I decided not to cancel the convention. I thank God that everything was successful.

I can never thank the thousands of AMVETS in Ohio and around the country for their courtesy, friendship and enthusiasm selflessly given throughout that year. I also want to thank you for the hundreds of gifts, gubernatorial and mayoral proclamations and the key to so many cities. These memories will never be forgotten.

Thomas J. McDonough. I am deeply grateful for the confidence you placed in me by electing me your national commander. With God's help and the guidance and assistance of AMVETS everywhere, we look forward to a good year . . . . I ask you to continue in the same spirit initiated by my predecessor that we rededicate ourselves to God and country, and to the principles upon which AMVETS was founded. The national officers elected to serve with me and I ask for your support . . . . Service to the veteran and his family will continue to be [the] number one priority.

—THE NATIONAL AMVET

DEC. 7, 1980

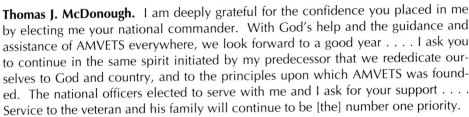

Frank D. Ruggiero. During my tenure, the NEC and I arranged for the sale of the AMVETS National Headquarters building on Rhode Island Avenue in Washington, D.C. We also purchased the land in Lanham, Md., where the present AMVET headquarters is located.

Another highlight was my trip to the Philippines, where I visited Corregidor, Bataan and Leyte—locations where major battles took place with the Japanese. My trip was hosted by the Philippine Government. Their hospitality was outstanding.

The best part of my term were the relationships developed with the many fine AMVETS and auxiliary members in the United States. I made many friends—all of whom I cherish today.

Bob Wilbraham was state commander of Ohio at the time of my administration. I'm sure he'll never forget the post we visited in the hinterlands of Ohio, with the temperature only 10 degrees and snowdrifts up to 10 feet high.

National Commanders

Ted Leszkiewicz. When we received a mandate from delegates to the national convention in Milwaukee, Wis., in August 1978, to pursue the possibility of constructing a national headquarters in Metropolitan Washington, I appointed an 18-man building committee of AMVETS experienced in real estate.

After three appraisals by qualified realtors, the estimated value of our old building stood at $700,000 as a fair market value to sell. After an on-site inspection of comparable property, I decided that the property was worth a million dollars, less selling commission.

Joe Ramsey and I did some special investigating with certain agents and were able to negotiate a $950,000 cash deal—no commission. We then sent committee chairman Earl Wright to locate suitable property in Virginia, Washington, D.C., or Maryland. Our present site in Lanham, Md., was chosen, even though the area was still considered the boondocks.

I spent my evenings laying out the preliminary design and floor plans of the building that pretty much remains the same. We searched out three construction bids with an appointed architect and put together a $1,800,000 financial package that was extremely beneficial to AMVETS.

As the year continued, I perceived a need to have a permanent liaison interacting with members of Congress, so I created a Legislative Action Committee.

At a special function of the Veterans Administration, I was greatly impressed by the number of volunteers contributing across the country and we immediately organized the original VAVS Committee under PNC Dante Spagnolo. Today, I would say it is the greatest "read-out" we have into the hospitals.

I created and developed the film version of the original "AMVETS Story." It has since been up-dated to a regular TV presentation. I also designed the "AMVET Joe" recruiting poster used as a vehicle for new membership/program development.

In between writing articles for *Stars and Stripes* and other publications, I visited dozens of AMVET departments and posts, spoke to quite a few legislative bodies across the country, and represented AMVETS with my wife Ann at the World Federation of Veterans in Paris, France.

The most outstanding occasions of my career were the three visits I had to the White House. On one occasion, I was in a photo session with President Jimmie Carter. Another time, I participated in a discussion of the Salt II Treaty with cabinet members and, finally, there was a state dinner with more than 100 dignitaries. My fondest memory at the White House was discussing international affairs with Zbigniew Brzezinski.

Joseph R. Koralewski. Among the highlights of my year as national commander, was the opportunity to represent the AMVETS as a delegate to the World Veterans Federation meeting in Italy. We were able to exchange many viewpoints and develop resolutions to be submitted to the United Nations for consideration in preparing for peace throughout the world.

While in Rome, I was given an audience with the Pope, who extended his papal blessing. My biggest surprise came two days later when a package arrived from the Vatican. Inside were five handwritten papal blessings on parchment paper—one for each member of my family. That is a treasure I'll cherish for the rest of my life.

After I returned from Italy, I began the arduous task of seeking loans to finance the construction of the planned national headquarters building in Lanham, Md. With the help of Joe Ramsey, executive director of the national service foundation; Earl Wright, chairman of the building committee; and Julius Pollatschek, our legal counsel; I was able to get a very favorable loan after weeks of tough negotiations.

A formal groundbreaking ceremony, attended by many city and state dignitaries, was held in December 1979.

Together with the commanders of the VFW and the American Legion, I also made many appeals to the Carter administration to consider elevating the VA to cabinet-level status. This battle was to continue for another eight years before VA finally achieved that status.

Other highlights of my year were the trips to Korea, Japan and the Philippines, where we presented then-President [Ferdinand] Marcos with a copy of the AMVETS resolutions, adopted at our previous convention. The resolutions supported the request of the Filipino people for continued economic and military aid.

The rest of the year was spent focusing on our ability to serve veterans and their families and developing community programs, such as the Special Olympics bowling tournaments, with which I am still very much involved.

Ernest F. Pitochelli. To all of the AMVETS and all of the auxiliary members, thank you for allowing me to serve as your national commander this year . . . . I would like to leave you with these few words. This is a veteran speaking: "Yes, America, you are beautiful. You told me and my fellow veterans that if I only tried to do my part, you would give me the satisfaction of a free life. And now the veteran of this country is sometimes overlooked and ignored." So our job as a veterans organization is to see that this never happens. —*Welcoming Message, 37th National Convention*

Donald R. Russell. We in AMVETS should be proud of . . . our recent accomplishments. The legislative package presented to Congress was well received and should be a help to all veterans. Our NEC meeting and Silver Helmet Banquet was . . . a huge success. The dedication of our newest carillon at Freedoms Foundation in Valley Forge, Pa., was well attended and an inspiring ceremony. Membership is increasing . . . and we are moving forward. AMVETS has the greatest potential for growth of any veterans organization, but it will take a concentrated effort by all of our members. —*The National AMVET*

Robert Martin. Shortly after I assumed office on Sept. 1, 1982, my finance officer, Claude DeBruhl, died of a heart attack. He was instrumental in helping AMVETS acquire its first computer system at national headquarters and the foundation.

The month had not yet ended when I welcomed the president of the Republic of the Philippines, Ferdinand E. Marcos, at the Sheraton Washington Hotel. President Marcos was awarded a medal for his courageous wartime service with the Armed Forces in the Far East. We also took this time to reaffirm our friendship and commitment to the Filipino people. Later in my term, I flew to the Philippines and presented the AMVETS Silver Helmet to President Marcos at his presidential residence.

Later in the fall, I was proud to be involved as AMVETS pledged its support for the speedy immigration of Amerasian children. Also at this time, the Vietnam Veterans Memorial was dedicated, with a parade to honor Vietnam veterans.

In December I traveled to Pearl Harbor to dedicate a new carillon on the U.S.S. *Arizona* Memorial. Before the month ended, I also traveled to Nice, France, to represent AMVETS at the World Veterans Federation conference.

National Commanders

In March I presented the AMVETS legislative agenda to Congress. We were sincere in our efforts to have Congress act on the Agent Orange issue and to stop the bureaucratic foot-dragging that appeared to be going on. I was extremely gratified to have Louisiana Senators Russell Long and Lindy Boggs in attendance with me.

In April I traveled to the Republic of China, to attend a VACRS [Vocational Assistance Commission to Retired Servicemen] conference. When I returned, it was time for the Silver Helmet Awards Banquet held at the Baltimore Hilton Hotel. The highlight of the banquet was the introduction of the "Angels of Bataan and Corregidor," special nurses who had been prisoners of war on Bataan.

The national convention was one of the last highlights of my term in office. It was held in New Orleans, where many AMVETS came out. Secretary of Labor Raymond J. Donovan was our keynote speaker and movie star Dom DeLuise was present to show support for the Amerasian children programs.

Robert L. Wilbraham. During my term, there were many items of importance, not only nationally, but for the organization as well.

It was mandated at the August 1983 convention that another attempt be made to petition Congress to open the AMVETS charter to accept all honorably discharged veterans or those who were presently serving. As the national commander, I felt this was a serious mandate and personally went to Congress. I talked "nose to nose" with 43 senators and 132 congressmen to explain AMVETS position on the bill that was pending in both houses of Congress. It was then sent to a committee, but was to be readdressed by Congress. At that time, the bill was reintroduced and it passed both the Senate and the House without a dissenting vote.

Another event that took place when I was national commander was the bombing of the Marine Corps Headquarters, adjacent to the airport in Beirut, Lebanon. At the time of the bombing, we were called by the USO in Washington and asked to attend a meeting in their offices with representatives from all the major veterans groups. The Red Cross had received an offer from World Airways to fly families of the wounded Marines over to Germany, free of charge, so that they could visit their loved ones in hospitals at Landstuhl and Wiesbaden. In a nutshell, World Airways would fly two members of any family to Frankfurt, Germany, from either San Francisco, Kansas City, or Baltimore.

We contacted a Marine Corps liaison officer to find out what arrangements could be made by the military to house these dependents. World Airways flew many pairs of dependents on three separate flights to Frankfurt and back. AMVETS, working together with the U.S. Marine Corps in Frankfurt, was able to obtain transportation for the families to the two hospitals for the visits, which were unrestricted, and give them free housing and food for the length of their stay. We also contacted the Marriott Hotel in our headquarters area, who supplied rooms and meals, free of charge, for up to two days, to anyone flying in for this purpose.

The next problem we faced was obtaining passports. With help from a Mr. Edgar and his staff, we were able to take all the dependents who did not have passports to the congressional passport office in downtown Washington. Nobody had to wait more than 2-1/2 hours to have a complete passport processed and be taken back to the hotel for the flight to Europe. At that same time, Kim Baker, our public relations director, assembled hundreds of tee shirts, toiletries and other items that could be used by the Marines in Beirut for distribution. We made arrangements with World Airways to fly all the materials to Beirut free of charge.

Reflections

John S. Lorec. To attain the position of national commander of AMVETS was the greatest honor that I could ever receive.

So many memories are still thought of daily. I will always remember the many state and post visits. This is where it all begins and all those involved in making those visits a success should be commended for their efforts.

The visits to the Philippines and VACRS [Vocational Assistance Commission for Retired Servicemen] in Taiwan were most exciting—from reviewing the troops to addressing VACRS delegates.

A very chilling experience for me was placing a wreath at the Tomb of the Unknowns at Arlington National Cemetery. Inaugural Week in 1985 was hectic. I attended many balls and receptions, but I will always remember the breakfast that AMVETS hosted for America's Medal of Honor recipients. To be among a group of heroes such as these was the greatest feeling. They were so humble and appreciative—but I don't know why! I believe that we should have been the ones who were humble and appreciative.

Robert A. Medairos. At the very beginning of my term . . . I said, "All we ask is that America be as faithful to its veterans as they were to America" . . . . you can imagine my thrill at having Sen. Ted Kennedy . . . declare that "the agenda of AMVETS should be the agenda of the whole nation" . . . . Also this year we accomplished a great deal in expressing our support for President Reagan's firm stance against communist tyranny . . . . The trip that inspired me the most was the one . . . to New York Harbor to witness the spectacular ceremonies surrounding the Statue of Liberty.   —*Annual Report, 42nd National Convention*

APR. 29, 1936–JAN. 10, 1991

Joseph T. Piening. I must tell you what a privilege it has been for me to serve in this position and how deeply grateful I am for the warm welcome and firm support I have received from you throughout our great land. I have done my utmost to help AMVETS grow larger and stronger; and while we've taken some strides forward, the task is far from complete and we must constantly rededicate ourselves to it.

—*The National AMVET*

James B. King. The past year has been one with a multitude of ups and downs as we've striven to maintain our membership levels, expand our participation at all levels of our community programs, and increase AMVETS exposure throughout the country . . . . One of the highlights has been the continued success of the AMVETS-sponsored "For Veterans Only" television program . . . . Our VAVS program remains strong as evidenced by the reactions to "Because We Care Day". . . . And I have seen . . . programs sponsored by individual posts which help serve their communities and further the ideals of Americanism.   —*The National AMVET*

National Commanders

Jimmy T. Smith. I have been fortunate during the past year to see how the legislative process works on a national level. Whatever one might think about how slowly these wheels turn in Washington sometimes, the fact is there is a system in place we should not take for granted . . . . the new Department of Veterans Affairs is proof . . . . The months have gone by quickly . . . . One of the highlights was the Silver Helmet Awards Banquet and the opportunity I had to honor a group of outstanding Americans. Similarly, you've given me the opportunity to serve you. It's been an honor I'll never forget.

— *THE NATIONAL AMVET*

Warren W. Eagles, Sr. After AMVETS' largest turnout for a national convention in years at Grand Rapids, Mich., my dreams became reality when I was elected national commander of this great organization. My only concern was my ability to live up to the expectations of the delegates.

The first week of September I enjoyed three rewarding days at the Freedoms Foundation with our essay winners and Junior AMVETS. The time was well spent as staff members of the foundation and AMVETS laid the groundwork for a long-term relationship between our two organizations.

That year, Hurricane Hugo came ashore in South Carolina and we received a request for assistance from our local AMVETS. National headquarters, with the help of the national service foundation, raised money, food and clothing from our posts throughout the country to send to the Department of South Carolina.

In early October, I attended the NSO seminar in New Orleans and saw firsthand the 45 men and women who represent AMVETS on a daily basis, attending classes, workshops and discussing programs. Before leaving Louisiania, I made my way north to Michigan for my first official department tour.

In November, I shared the podium with Secretary of Labor Elizabeth Dole, Under Secretary Tom Collins, Secretary of Veterans Affairs Ed Derwinski and singer Lee Greenwood at the Eighth Annual Salute to All-American Veterans. I led the gathering in the Pledge of Allegiance. Soon after, I had the pleasure of representing AMVETS on Veterans Day at Arlington National Cemetery.

To begin the new year, I toured more than 50 posts in Ohio, made many personal appearances and attended the department's mid-winter conference. Then it was off to North Carolina, New Jersey, Illinois and California. Upon returning to headquarters, I visited with Secretary Derwinski to discuss issues such as Agent Orange and the VA system. Later, I participated in the National Salute to Hospitalized Veterans at the VA medical center in Hampton, Va.

One of my most memorable trips was to the Far East, accompanied by my wife Donna and National Auxiliary President Jean Baxter and her husband Tom. We visited the American Institute in Taiwan as well as with the generals and staff at the Vocational Assistance Commission for Retired Servicemen, mayors, businessmen and the vice premier of Taiwan.

Our next stop was Seoul, Korea, where there were many demonstrations at the college next to our hotel and throughout our tours in South Korea. The highlight of our trip was a visit to the DMZ (demilitarized zone).

On the way back home, we stopped in Hawaii and were briefed at the Joint Casualty Resolution Center on how remains from Korea and Vietnam are identified. We also met with officials from the *Arizona* Memorial and the National Cemetery of the Pacific, where we laid wreaths.

Vaughn L. Brown, Sr. President Bush spoke of a "Thousand Points of Light," but in four years' time, he was unable to come up with that number. If he had traveled with me, he would have surpassed it, in one year, by 10,000.

We would have traveled to the 36 states I visited, beginning with Michigan, extending from Maine to Alaska and then on to Texas and Florida. I would then show him what our members are doing for the veterans and their communities.

I would also have taken the president to the VA medical centers in those states so that he could see what our volunteers are doing and hear the praise from the hospital management and staff for the contributions they made. Then he would have observed the dedication of our staff members towards the care of their veteran patients. We would have also visited some of our national service officers so that the president could personally observe the kinds of assistance our NSOs have offered to veterans.

In South Carolina, the president would have attended the Special Olympics and caught a glimpse of AMVETS community service in action. Elsewhere, he would have attended programs in a Catholic school in Washington and a public school in New Jersey dedicated to patriotism and Americanism.

In Alaska and Connecticut, local posts were named for and dedicated to servicepersons who had lost their lives in Operation DESERT STORM. And in Indiana, he would have attended the dedication of an AMVET carillon at the VA cemetery in Marion. A visit to the Ohio Veterans Children's Home and the School for Veterans in Scotland, Pa., would have shown him that AMVETS cares not only about the veteran but also his dependents.

A trip to Parris Island, S.C., where we sat in the reviewing stand for the graduation of the Marine Corps recruits or to Great Lakes Naval Center, where I had the honor of reviewing the graduation class, would have inspired him to see the dedication of our young men and women to the welfare of their country.

At the Welcome Home Celebration in our nation's capital, 10,000 DESERT STORM troops (10,000 "points of light") paraded past the presidential reviewing stand where I had the honor of sitting with dignitaries and other veterans representatives.

Finally, I would have taken him on a tour of AMVETS National Headquarters and National Service Foundation so that he could see where all the above originates—thanks to the work of dedicated staff.

James L. Singler. Several important things happened during my term in office. One of them was the 50th anniversary of the bombing of Pearl Harbor. I was at the U.S.S. *Arizona* Memorial when President George Bush gave his address.

A few weeks after my visit to Hawaii, my testimonial dinner was held in Columbus, Ohio. After that, I went on a tour of the state, then visited Texas, Michigan, Ohio, Massachusetts, Virginia, Illinois, Wisconsin and California.

In January, PNC Ralph Hall and I visited California to meet with the Toyota U.S.A. representatives about the development of the Safe Driving Challenge Program. Toyota agreed to join in our efforts to establish the program. We began publicizing it to the departments so they would be ready to go along with the idea. We had quite a problem because Toyota was not an American-named car, but our hard work paid off. The convention approved using Toyota for the SDC.

The most controversial situation I experienced during my term was the plan to use two VA hospitals—one in Tuskeegee, Ala., and the other in Salem, Va—to treat nonveterans. We decided to go against VA on this matter and publicized our concerns. Not long afterwards, the matter was dropped—thanks to all veterans who wrote letters and did what they could to show that this was not the way to operate a VA hospital.

National Commanders

Another positive thing that occurred while I was in office was the beginning of our newsletter, AMVET WORLD. It has been well received by everybody and I think it's an ideal piece of communication from National to the different posts.

We worked on membership for the year and began a promotion campaign in Texas. The Department of Texas helped us with the funding for the program and we got some new members from it, but not as many as we thought we would.

Our annual convention was held in Orlando, Fla. We had a little scare while we were down there when Hurricane Andrew swept through southern Florida. Because of the hurricane, we didn't have as many attendees as we hoped. It was a very successful convention, however, and one of the few where we made money.

James J. Kenney. When I was elected national commander, I knew I would be faced with many challenges, and one quickly surfaced after my election. For the first time in 12 years AMVETS had to readjust to a shift in U.S. presidents. Even so, I felt it was of utmost importance to develop a productive relationship with the Clinton administration in order to maintain AMVETS goals.

Inauguration Week was something to behold. I attended the VFW dinner dance where I first met President Clinton and his wife, as well as Vice President Gore and his wife. The next day AMVETS held its Congressional Medal of Honor Recipients breakfast with more than 400 people in attendance. I also attended the Joint Chiefs of Staff luncheon and the American Legion dinner.

A few weeks later, I met with The Normandy Foundation in New York City to kick off the Wall of Liberty; then I was off to California to meet with Toyota USA about our Safe Driving Challenge Program. The next several months were filled with tours as well as meetings in Washington, D.C., with Secretary Jesse Brown, Senators Jay Rockefeller and Barbara McKulski and our long-time friend Congressman Sonny Montgomery.

There are many memories I will always cherish, but one of the highlights of my year was testifying before the Senate and House Veterans' Affairs Committees. The feeling I had afterwards cannot be expressed. Another great moment of many was the Silver Helmet Awards banquet, attended by a record number of AMVETS.

I also had the privilege of dedicating two new carillons—one in Indiana and the other in North Carolina. Contributions of the service foundation and departments involved helped to make the dedication services a success. My trips to Taiwan and Korea were a gratifying experience, too. Both the Vocational Assistance Commission for Retired Servicemen in Taiwan and the Korean Veterans Association take pride in assisting their veterans in many areas.

When I began my term, I promised 125 percent of dedication to the job. I visited 27 states, more than 25 percent of post homes, 12 VA medical centers and six state veterans homes and attended dozens of government meetings in the Washington area. I believe I can truly say that I lived up to my promise.

Donald M. Hearon. As I look back on my year as national commander, it is one I'll always remember. So many memories. One of my most vivid is a conversation I had with the mayor of St. Lo in Normandy. During the war, 80 percent of the town was destroyed. He told me that you never appreciate freedom so much as when you have it then lose it. "We lost homes," he said, "but the Americans lost lives." Listening to the mayor express his appreciation for what our people did over there was a lesson in patriotism I'll never forget.

With the opportunity to do extensive travel—visiting posts and departments and going overseas to represent AMVETS—I met so many great people. This stands out as the highlight of my term. Like commanders before me, I had a chance to go to Taiwan as a guest of VACRS [Vocational Assistance Commission for Retired Servicemen], with a stopoff in Hawaii. There, I was briefed by the Joint Task Force-Full Accounting on the POW/MIA situation in Vietnam. Later, I was able to go there in person as part of a special presidential commission.

Then, of course, there was the 50th anniversary of D-Day. Seeing so many veterans who gave so much back then really drove home to me what it means to be a patriot. I'll never forget when the president asked them all to stand and be recognized. It was a moving experience, and something I'll always cherish.

Reflecting on all that has happened to me, I realize, again, that it was people who made it possible—from those who elected me and have supported me throughout the year to the many new friends and acquaintances I've made.

Geremia *continued from page 65*

We knew that a single vote in the Senate against it would doom our hopes. Neveretheless, we were satisfied with the press we were receiving, and we were confident that we were out from the shadows of the other veterans organizations.

During the summer of 1947, I became the neighbor of Sen. J. Howard McGrath, a very close associate of President Truman's. McGrath had heard of AMVETS, and I felt with his backing and connection to the president, we could go a long way toward getting our charter approved by the Senate. The two of us became good friends, then I told him about what we had to go through to get the charter. After hearing what I had to say, McGrath was more than willing to help; he said he would be going to Washington in a few days and would see what he could do.

McGrath talked with Truman and apparently the president liked what he heard about AMVETS, because he drew up a plan to promote the charter to the Senate. When the session was over, the charter legislation passed with the unanimous vote it needed. Many other AMVET members worked hard to get this approval and no doubt this was very helpful, but I think the work McGrath did with President Truman was paramount. On the House side, it was Francis E. Walters from Pennsylvania who sponsored the bill. Ray Sawyer, Elliot Newcomb, Clarence Adamy and others lobbied furiously to help get the charter legislation passed.

Another major boost for the organization was the formation of the national service foundation. Harold Keats was appointed as administrator and he worked tirelessly to find ways of raising funds for AMVETS.

The next high point came when Harold Russell was elected national commander in 1949. He did something that very few people seem to know about. President Truman was attempting to unify the Armed Forces under one department but was having great difficulty getting the services to even consider it. So he invited Harold and his staff to the White House to talk with these groups.

When we walked into the East Room, we were escorted to where most of the activity was going on. In one corner of the room was all the Navy brass; in the other, all the Army brass. As Harold approached the gathering with that big smile of his, he raised both his hooks and said, "Gentlemen, Shall we shake hands?" There was a slight pause; then the two heads of these military groups rushed toward Harold and grabbed his hooks. Needless to say, we left the White House feeling that perhaps President Truman would succeed in unifying the Armed Forces.

Obviously, during this period there were others who contributed enormously to the success of AMVETS. I'm happy to say they shared the dreams of the founders about the organization's aims and purposes.

Albert C. Geremia resides in Rhode Island and is the surviving founder of AMVETS.

When & Where

Term	Commander	President	Convention
1944–45	Elmo W. Keel*		
1945–46	Jack W. Hardy*		Chicago
1946–47	Ray Sawyer	Edith G. Males*	St. Louis
1947–48	Edgar C. Corry, Jr.*	Kathryn N. Snyder*	Columbus
1948–49	Harold A. Keats	Adeline P. Fogg*	Chicago
1949–50	Harold S. Russell	Evelyn Lauritson*	Des Moines
1950–51	Harold S. Russell	Evelyn M. Flasco*	Cleveland
1951–52	John L. Smith*	Dorothy Sullivan	Boston
1952–53	Marshall E. Miller	Darline Gordon*	Grand Rapids
1953–54	Henry J. Mahady*	Beatrice F. Russell	Indianapolis
1954–55	Rufus H. Wilson	Ruth K. Nickerson*	Miami
1955–56	Rudolph G. Pesata*	Florence B. Stripe	Philadelphia
1956–57	Dominick L. Strada*	Gloria I. Clark	Milwaukee
1957–58	Stuart J. Satullo	June L. Miller	Boston
1958–59	Winston E. Burdine*	Mae Boone*	St. Louis
1959–60	Harold T. Berc	Aldean M. Sorrells	Grand Rapids
1960–61	Harold S. Russell	Lucia C. Russo	Miami Beach
1961–62	Edwin P. Fifielski*	Anne E. Hall	Louisville
1962–63	Dante E. Spagnolo	Alice Oana	New York City
1963–64	Edmund M. Gulewicz*	Leah Monasterio*	Detroit
1964–65	Lincoln S. Tamraz	Marie Redden	Philadelphia
1965–66	Ralph E. Hall	Jewel W. Fifielski	Boston
1966–67	A. Leo Anderson	Ellen Bogatay	Columbus
1967–68	Anthony J. Caserta*	Rita Potvin	Hollywood
1968–69	Joseph V. Ferrino	Kathleen Hengely*	New Orleans
1969–70	Robert B. Gomulinski*	Marie Miller	Detroit
1970–71	Robert W. Showalter	Betty Torner	New York City
1971–72	Joe F. Ramsey, Jr.	Dorothy M. LeRoy	Los Angeles
1972–73	Joseph R. Sanson*	Doris L. Burdine	New Orleans
1973–74	Berge Avadanian	Dorothy Bussard Ruph	St. Louis
1974–75	Essley B. Burdine*	Grace G. Osborn	Hollywood
1975–76	Paul C. Welsh	Toni Gomulinski	Des Moines
1976–77	Thomas J. McDonough*	Doris G. Shrake	Philadelphia
1977–78	Frank D. Ruggiero	Pearl V. Barnett*	Atlantic City
1978–79	Ted Leszkiewicz	Jane Ashley	Milwaukee
1979–80	Joseph R. Koralewski	Lila B. Longworth*	Cleveland
1980–81	Ernest F. Pitochelli	Anne Brown	Dallas
1981–82	Donald R. Russell	Margaret Rummel	Louisville
1982–83	Robert Martin	Ruth Singler	Hollywood
1983–84	Robert L. Wilbraham	Agnes P. Kolano	New Orleans
1984–85	John S. Lorec	Betty M. Wineland	Knoxville
1985–86	Robert A. Medairos*	Mary S. Barrow	Baltimore
1986–87	Joseph T. Piening	Sylvia Lipowski	Cincinnati
1987–88	James B. King	Dorothy J. Stoddard	St. Louis
1988–89	Jimmy T. Smith	Betty J. Leisure*	Albuquerque
1989–90	Warren W. Eagles, Sr.	Jean Baxter	Grand Rapids
1990–91	Vaughn L. Brown, Sr.	Nita I. Cornell	Atlanta
1991–92	James L. Singler	Dorothy R. Bull	Louisville
1992–93	James J. Kenney	Betty S. Lawson	Orlando
1993–94	Donald M. Hearon	Barbara S. Hinsley	New Orleans

*deceased

DECEASED

Edith G. Males. Taken at the conclusion of the organizational meeting of the auxiliary on a national level, [a photograph] shows the first officers of the National Department. It is an occasion to be particularly proud of because it was our beginning and these women, newly elected to office, were the trail blazers—the pioneers of everything good in [the] AMVETS Auxiliary.　　　*—AMVETS 25th Anniversary Book*

DECEASED

Kathryn N. Snyder. Setting up the national auxiliary headquarters is always a big task; in our second year of existence, it was a real adventure.

The auxiliary headquarters was in Champaign, Ill., where the AMVETS Department of Illinois had loaned us the space. We will always be grateful for their generosity. Charter applications were pouring in, so we divided our time between signing them and arranging work space.　　　*—AMVETS 25th Anniversary Book*

DECEASED

Adeline P. Fogg. Adeline is an impressive speaker. She carried the meaning and importance of Americanism to auxiliaries across the country.

—AMVETS 25th Anniversary Book

DECEASED

Evelyn Lauritson. The highlight of my year was the dedication of AMVETS' first carillon at Arlington National Cemetery. President Truman was there and my escort was the Honorable Carlos P. Romulo, ambassador of the Philippines.

—AMVETS 25th Anniversary Book

National Presidents

Evelyn M. Flasco. During her year in office, the "Battle of the Budget"—money and taxes—were very much on the minds of the young World War II veterans. Evie was attuned to the times and hearing her speak of national problems helped many auxiliary members realize that women had an important role to help our country through AMVETS and its auxiliary.   —*AMVETS 25th Anniversary Book*

DECEASED

Dorothy Sullivan. In April 1952, the new AMVETS headquarters in Washington, D.C., was dedicated. I was pleased to present the auxiliary. Our members were proud of this achievement by the parent organization. I remember enjoying a pleasant conversation with President Harry S. Truman in the headquarters building after the ceremonies.   —*AMVETS 25th Anniversary Book*

Darline Gordon. The auxiliary was rapidly gaining national recognition, I was extremely proud to present a life membership to Mrs. Harry S. Truman on Nov. 11, 1952. That's one Veterans Day I'll always remember.   —*AMVETS 25th Anniversary Book*

DECEASED

Beatrice F. Russell. Veterans around the world share many similar problems and I enjoyed the opportunity to exchange ideas with representatives of the World Veterans Federation at a reception held in the National Press Club, Washington, D.C. . . . It was rewarding to learn that Mrs. Richard Nixon and Alfred G. Vanderbilt . . . were extremely interested in the service programs of our auxiliary.   —*AMVETS 25th Anniversary Book*

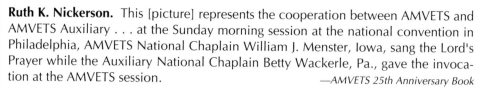

DECEASED

Ruth K. Nickerson. This [picture] represents the cooperation between AMVETS and AMVETS Auxiliary . . . at the Sunday morning session at the national convention in Philadelphia, AMVETS National Chaplain William J. Menster, Iowa, sang the Lord's Prayer while the Auxiliary National Chaplain Betty Wackerle, Pa., gave the invocation at the AMVETS session. —*AMVETS 25th Anniversary Book*

Florence B. Stripe. As a founder of the National AMVETS Auxiliary, it was my distinct pleasure to serve as auxiliary national president during the year 1955-56.

The organization was still young and growing, and membership was an important part of our program. All of the varied programs of the auxiliary were successfully carried out. Auxiliaries all across the country mined for silver (money, that is) for the National Polio Foundation. I was privileged to attend the meeting of The National Polio Foundation in California when Dr. Jonas Salk announced to the world the availability of the Salk vaccine.

June Miller wrote the Code of An American Mother as an Americanism project. This code was recognized by Freedoms Foundation with a presentation of the George Washington Medal for Excellence. Later, the code was written into the *Congressional Record.*

This was the one and only year that a national president was invited by AMVETS to give testimony on the War Orphans Scholarship Bill before the Veterans Committee of the House of Representatives .

I represented the national auxiliary at all conferences, conventions and workshops that I was invited to attend. —*AMVETS 25th Anniversary Book*

Gloria I. Clark. The March of Dimes has always received outstanding support from AMVETS auxiliaries. This is one of the many ways in which our members serve their communities in the name of our organization. The 1957 March of Dimes Poster Girl was Marlene Olsen, age 4-1/2, from Boston, Mass. She captured our hearts when National Commander Dominick Strada and I were photographed with her. —*AMVETS 25th Anniversary Book*

June L. Miller. AMVETS Auxiliary did many things during 1957-58. One of the most rewarding was participating in the AMVETS American Bookshelf program. We understood how important books are in making friends across the seas. —*AMVETS 25th Anniversary Book*

National Presidents

Mae Boone. National President Mae Boone presented the first copy of "Young America's Creed" to Gov. Clinton Clauson in the state house in Augusta [Ga.], when the Department of Maine launched the Americanism program destined to place copies of the creed in every classroom in the state's public and parochial schools. Mae was carrying on the tradition of national presidents to help state departments and local auxiliaries obtain . . . publicity for their special projects.

—AMVETS 25th Anniversary Book

DECEASED

Aldean M. Sorrells. The auxiliary is happy to share in the AMVETS Carillon Program. We do this by providing maintenance for the . . . carillons. It was my honor to represent our members at the dedication ceremonies of the AMVETS carillon at the site of the U.S.S. *Arizona* Memorial, a hallowed place to veterans of World War II. *—AMVETS 25th Anniversary Book*

Lucia C. Russo. Assistance to the mentally retarded was the prime project during my term. AMVETS Post 29 and its auxiliary in Poplar Bluff, Mo., was instrumental in establishing a local training center for the mentally retarded in their community. I was most happy to tour the facility when I visited the Missouri Department. It was a revelation to observe the marvelous techniques used in the rehabilitation of the children there for this special training. *—AMVETS 25th Anniversary Book*

Anne E. Hall. On Aug. 27, 1961, in Louisville, Ky., I was elected the 16th national president of the AMVETS Auxiliary. There were many highlights during the following 12 months.

Civil defense was a national focus, and personal preparedness became the "watchwords." I joined in promoting the Home Fallout Shelter Program by having a shelter constructed at my home. It supported all features—emergency pantry, sleeping accommodations, and an air-filtering system.

Although the public acceptance of auto seat belts was just beginning, I participated in presenting belts to governors and city officials. From the Old North Church in Boston to the World's Fair in Seattle, these messages were publicized.

December 7, 1961, was the 20th Anniversary of the bombing of Pearl Harbor. It was an emotional day because I helped place a wreath at the Tomb of the Unknowns in Arlington National Cemetery. Then I attended the Women's Forum on National Security in Washington, which illustrated the role women assumed in the goal to "inform and arouse interest in national security."

On Mar. 31, 1962, the Fifth Annual Silver Helmet Awards banquet was held at the Mayflower Hotel in Washington, D.C. Recipients included Eleanor Roosevelt, J.

Edgar Hoover, Sen. Everett Dirkson, and the Mercury astronauts, while Sen. Edmund Muskie served as toastmaster. An impressive roster indeed! Of course, each visit to Washington gave me another opportunity to visit auxiliary headquarters at 1710 Rhode Island Avenue.

The trip to Hawaii to participate in the dedication of the U.S.S. *Arizona* Memorial was certainly a trip that I will never forget. The gleaming white structure, the ringing of the carillon bells, the seeping-oil Pacific waters and the shadowy outline of the sunken ship set the stage for the impressive ceremony.

During my tenure, membership in the auxiliary grew: 30 local auxiliary and two department charters were issued. Then on Aug. 26, 1962, I adjourned the national convention in New York City and completed my term. I had traveled some 44,000 miles visiting departments in the four corners of the country—Maine to Florida, California to Washington—and the states in between. I visited historical sites, hospitals and schools and participated in parades, celebrations and dinners. But without a doubt, the most valued memory I have are those of the friendships I made all across the nation during my year as national president.

Alice Oana. [The] AMVETS Auxiliary willingly cooperates with other service organizations in work and on special occasions. It gave me special pleasure to represent our members at the groundbreaking ceremony at the Cathedral of the Pines, Rindge, N.H., for a memorial bell tower honoring all American women who died for our country in war-time service. The ceremony was held Memorial Day 1963.

—*AMVETS 25th Anniversary Book*

Leah Monasterio. AMVETS Auxiliary members had a special feeling for the wives of the seven [Mercury] astronauts. We admired their dignity in the trying period of waiting during the space shots. We remembered that we, too, had waited while our husbands served our country. It was my privilege to present the Auxiliary Distinquished Service Award to these courageous women. It was the first award given collectively to the seven wives. The presentations were made in Washington.

—*AMVETS 25th Anniversary Book*

DECEASED

Marie Redden. My main memories are of the wonderful people that I met and the many friends that I made. Among my highlights were serving as hostess for the national commander when he entertained members of the Senate at the Mayflower Hotel; placing a wreath on the Tomb of the Unknown Soldier on Veterans Day; placing a wreath at the tomb of Herbert Hoover at the time of his interment in West Branch, Iowa; riding in the St. Patrick's Day parade in Boston; and having lunch with Governor John Volpe in Philadelphia.

Some of the special programs that we were participating in were Shoes for the Shoeless; the Tidy Tots program; and a nationwide letter-writing effort to Lady Bird Johnson, asking her to intervene in the closing of various VA hospitals.

Freedoms Foundation was accepted as one of our projects and I had the privilege of visiting Valley Forge and the foundation, which was then being constructed.

Later, in my term, misunderstandings arose within the posts and at national headquarters between the Auxiliary and AMVETS. I made a special effort to cooperate with AMVETS and succeeded in forming a very harmonious relationship before my year was completed. I still count many AMVETS as my good friends.

Jewel W. Fifielski. With the theme "AMVETS Auxiliary for Freedoms Foundation," I promoted funds for Freedom Bricks during my year. Auxiliary members launched a campaign to support the Foundation . . . to help preserve and perpetuate the American Way of Life. Over $7,500 was raised for the Alexander Hamilton Residence Hall at the foundation . . . I am very proud of the response.

—AMVETS 25th Anniversary Book

Ellen Bogatay. A national president realizes that the honor accorded her by state and city officials during her travels is but a reflection of the great respect our auxiliaries and posts have earned in their communities. *—AMVETS 25th Anniversary Book*

Rita Potvin. The national president never fully understands the impact of the work our members do until she tours their state. It is her function to give encouragement to the membership but this is a two-way street because she always leaves greatly inspired by the work she has seen. I was pleased to receive the key to the city of Springfield, Ill., presented by the mayor. *—AMVETS 25th Anniversary Book*

Kathleen Hengely. During my term of office, I participated in many service programs: hospital, carillon, child welfare, community service and Americanism. As I traveled across the country, I visited many of the VA hospitals and found our volunteers giving of their time and service. On the local level, fine work was being done in their communities and members were working for Americanism in many ways.

I was active in the All-American Conference to Combat Communism along with my commander, Joe Ferrino. Other affairs where I represented the auxiliary were the Woman's Forum on National Security and on the jury at Freedoms Foundation.

Each president has a special memory and mine is visiting the White House as a guest of President and Mrs. Johnson.

DECEASED

I attended a briefing at the Pentagon concerning the Vietnam War, which was of particular interest to me since our son was in Vietnam at the time.

At Commander Ferrino's testimonial in Boston, Mass., I had the opportunity to go aboard the U.S.S. *Massachusetts*, which was my first experience on a large ship. He and I traveled to many of the same posts and auxiliaries throughout our country. While on tour, we often met the governors, congressmen, senators, mayors and other important people of the states.

After serving the Department of Ohio as president in 1953-54, I went on to assume positions on the national level, including that of national executive secretary (1964-68) and editor of the *Auxiliary News* (1972-76). When I was elected president, I served under the theme "God Bless America, Let Freedom Ring." I felt this theme was what AMVETS was all about and certainly served as a wonderful topic for the addresses I gave to our auxiliaries.

Maria Miller. I believe for the second time in history, the national commander of AMVETS and the national president of the auxiliary were elected from the same state. Both National Commander Bob Gomulinski and I were from Michigan.

A year as national president can be filled with so many wonderful experiences and memories that it is hard to distinguish any particular one. One of the most impressionable experiences was an Americanism program developed by Cleveland Hill Elementary School in Cheektowaga, N.Y., so all children of our nation could recite the "Pledge of Allegiance" in unison. The students at this school had developed a table showing when all students would be in school at the same time.

The local auxiliary informed me of the program and I then participated with the children of East Kelloggsville Elementary School in Kentwood, Mich.

Memories of my year as national president will always be cherished and I am thankful Commander Gomulinski included me in many joint activities that year.

Betty Torner. A visit with the president of the United States, Richard M. Nixon, shall certainly be the highlight of my year. The commemorative pin he presented me shall always be a most treasured keepsake . . . . No matter where you happen to be, our members are working for the good of the organization. These members are the very same ones who bring joy, comfort and pleasure to many unfortunate persons in today's busy world.

—*THE NATIONAL AMVET*

Dorothy M. Leroy. During my year as national president of the AMVETS Auxiliary, I visited every state with auxiliaries and I had the pleasure of organizing the Department of Tennessee. My first official act included a trip to Hawaii to visit the U.S.S. *Arizona* Memorial where I laid a wreath.

In 1972, the auxiliary hosted the Women's Forum on National Security in Washington, D.C. The theme of the forum was "Americans Stand Up." At the conclusion of the forum was the presentation of the Molly Pitcher Award on national security to Texas industrialist H. Ross Perot. Another outstanding event was serving as a judge for the awards from Freedoms Foundation at Valley Forge.

On Veterans Day, it was an honor to participate in the wreath-laying ceremony at the Tomb of the Unknowns in Arlington National Cemetery. Then on Memorial

Day, I was privileged to spend time in Alaska to honor the servicemen and women lost at sea by tossing a wreath from the air into Cooks Inlet.

The 1972 national convention was held in New Orleans, La., where Past National President Leah Monasterio served as chairman. The New Orleans spirit was well represented with the national president's Hawaiian reception and the beautiful AMVETS and AMVETS Auxiliary Parade through the streets of New Orleans. My national commander, Joseph Ramsey, and I ended our year as stars of the "Rex" King and Queen Ball.

Doris L. Burdine. The year I was elected national president was the only one in AMVETS history where there wasn't a special Silver Helmet presentation at the mid-year National Executive Committee meeting. National Commander Joseph Sanson chose to present the Silver Helmet Awards during the national convention at the Chase-Park Plaza Hotel in St. Louis, Mo. The national auxiliary held its mid-year NEC meeting in Chicago in January 1973.

In that year, the national auxiliary had 24 departments, with a total of 414 local auxiliaries. The membership was 14,055, an increase of 646 over the prior year. I was pleased to visit all departments and many of the local auxiliaries in unorganized states. The auxiliary national headquarters was in Maine and I made several trips to visit our executive secretary and plan administrative affairs.

The auxiliary held membership in various organizations and I attended the Women's Forum on National Security; the Women's Committee on Employment of the Handicapped meeting in Washington, D.C.; the National Foundation Leadership Conference in New York City; the National Rehabilitation Counseling Association in San Juan; and the Veteran's Summit at Freedoms Foundation.

Today, I still serve the auxiliary as parliamentarian, department secretary/treasurer and VAVS representative, and treasurer of Auxiliary 1 in Atlanta, Ga.

Dorothy J. Bussard Ruph. Becoming a member of AMVETS Auxiliary to Post 9, Middletown, Md., in 1960 was the beginning of my career at AMVETS. I held all offices in my local post auxiliary, which was very active in the community, and volunteered many hours in veterans hospitals and nursing homes. I also took part in child welfare programs, patriotic and Americanism contests, and parades.

In 1965, the AMVETS Department of Maryland formed a state auxiliary, where I first held office as an NEC woman. I served in that capacity for many years and eventually held other offices within the department, including that of president. With the formation of the department, volunteerism doubled.

At the 1969 national convention in New York City, I ran for my first national office—national public relations officer. I was elected and later won all other offices I ran for, including national chaplain, junior vice president, state vice president and president.

It was during my year as national president that I was honored in the *Congressional Record.* Another highlight was the appeal I made to national officers to bring in new programs on the national level. Then at the 1974 national convention in Florida, the John Tracy Clinic Program (which continues to the present day) was brought in by Pearl Barnett, my national liaison officer.

I was very honored to have been chosen as Outstanding Member of the Year in 1969 by the Department of Maryland, Outstanding Woman of the Community in Middletown (1970) and Outstanding Woman of the Year in Maryland (1971).

Reflections

Reflections

Grace G. Osborn. The year I was elected national auxiliary president Essley Burdine was elected national commander. He was most considerate of the other subsidiary organizations, including Junior AMVETS, Sad Sacks and Sackettes, and he also kept me informed at all times.

During my year, a lot of time and effort went into studying and revising our bylaws. I also kept busy with groups and meetings. I started the Council of NEC Women. They met at the NECs and conventions to compare problems and successes, and discuss resolutions.

One unforgettable event was presenting a wreath at the Tomb of the Unknown Soldier at Arlington Cemetery. Another highlight was having tea at the White House with First Lady Betty Ford. Since President Gerald Ford was an AMVET from Michigan, we presented Mrs. Ford with an auxiliary membership.

The John Tracy Clinic for Deaf Children had been adopted as a program, but my year was really the first that we raised a lot of money for it.

The AMVETS Auxiliary was active in other programs such as the Women's Forum for National Security, which met in Washington, D.C., every January. At the meetings, I had the opportunity to meet the presidents of the other veterans organizations. Many of us took our congressmen as guests to the banquet.

Toni Gomulinski. I was elected on Aug. 17, 1975, at the 29th National Convention in Des Moines, Iowa.

The project I chose for my year was Freedoms Foundation, with "Freedom Is . . ." being my theme. The Spirit of '76 was everywhere in 1975. It was also the year the auxiliary celebrated its 30th anniversary.

That December 7 at Arlington Cemetery, AMVETS hosted the Veterans Day ceremonies and, needless to say, it was most impressive to be on stage with Commander Paul Welsh. He was very considerate of me and was the first commander to invite an auxiliary president on an oversees trip. Commander Welsh, his wife Betty, my husband Past National Commander Bob Gomulinski and myself visited Korea and the 38th parallel. It was a trip I shall never forget.

There are so many other great memories. For one, I'm proud to say that I was the first national president to present the National Humanitarian Auxiliary Award to Rep. Corinne C. (Lindy) Boggs of Louisiana. The award, at that time, consisted of a medallion with a ribbon in a shadow box. I designed the current award, which is a lucite replica of the Washington Monument with the medallion at the base.

The bicentennial year in AMVET Auxiliary history was a most successful one. The year ended with the national convention in Philadelphia, Pa., on Aug. 15, 1976—a fitting ending in the city where all our history began.

Doris G. Shrake. When I started my year in September 1976, I had many goals and ideas as most national presidents do. First of all, I was so proud to be a member and to have reached the status of president of such a worthwhile organization. One of my first obligations was to rejuvenate the state of Florida, which at that time, was struggling to stay alive. They have certainly excelled in all programs in the past several years and I'd like to think that I had a part in that growth.

At the national convention where I was elected, the John Tracy Clinic was brought to our attention. I chose to adopt the clinic as my project of the year and made the first presentation to Mrs. Spencer Tracy at the clinic in California. And at the convention in Atlantic City, I was extremely pleased to present our John Tracy Clinic family with the first donation from our organization and, 15 years later, to have that family stand before us again. It also was an honor to present Mrs. Tracy

National Presidents

with the Auxiliary Humanitarian Award at the Silver Helmet Banquet that year. Other highlights were meeting Ambassador Shirley Temple Black and President Gerald Ford, who was presented the AMVETS Gold Helmet at the White House.

Pearl V. Barnett. While serving as second vice president, Pearl proposed the national project to sponsor correspondence courses for pre-deaf children in cooperation with the John Tracy Clinic. "Working for America—Ocean to Ocean" was the theme she emphasized throughout her term, including the need to publicize programs of the Department of Labor to assist veterans with training and employment. She was a former editor of the *Auxiliary News.*   *—Auxiliary Archives*

DECEASED

Jane Ashley. As I traveled this great country, each of you has exemplified my theme this year "A Time of Challenge Togetherness, Involvement, Motivation and Enthusiasm . . . ." To Past National Commander Ted Leszkiewicz, my sincere thanks for your friendship and understanding. To each of you, thanks for the greatest opportunity during my lifetime—that of serving as your national president. Your friendliness and outstanding courtesies have made this the most memorable year of my life.   *—1979 Convention Journal*

Lila B. Longworth. Lila, a resident of Ohio, served opposite of National Commander Joseph R. Koralewski, also from the Buckeye State. The John Tracy Clinic was her special project. She selected as her slogan for the year "Working Together Because We Care" and stressed the need to publicize auxiliary programs throughout the country.   *—Auxiliary Archives*

DECEASED

Anne Brown. "A New Decade . . . A Time for Growth" was the slogan I chose for the year I served as national president. Since I worked at a state university, it was natural that I chose scholarships as my pet project.

Since Freedoms Foundation has always been a very special project to me; I suggested to Mr. Ramsey that the AMVETS National Service Foundation install a carillon there. It was completed after my year, but I was still very proud that day.

The Long Range Planning Committee was instituted on my recommendation, under the very capable leadership of PNP Maria Miller. In my opinion, this was an outstanding committee, working toward the continued success and growth of the national department and its programs.

During my term as national president, AMVETS moved from its headquarters at 1710 Rhode Island Avenue in Washington, to the current location in Lanham, Md.

It was a special privilege to participate with Commander Pitochelli in the dedication of the new headquarters. Little did I know then that I would later live at headquarters when my husband Vaughn served as national commander.

Margaret Rummel. As I look back over the year I was president, there were a few highlights of historical note. I was fortunate to be able to present the Auxiliary's Humanitarian Award to Joy Ufima, a nurse from Pennsylvania. It was also a pleasure to serve on the jury at Freedoms Foundation for the judging of their awards.

My theme for the year was "Pennies for Peggy," and I had pennies presented to me in every shape and manner. These pennies were used to support our service programs.

For me, it was a good year, because I had the opportunity to travel and meet many auxiliary members. I became very, very impressed with all their accomplishments. They were always willing to reach out to those who needed help. It was their constant generosity and their love for people that I will always remember.

Many times I have heard comments from directors of volunteers such as "the AMVETS Auxiliary—I don't have to worry, they know what they are doing" or "I wish I had the AMVETS Auxiliary in my area." These are great compliments to our members. While we often wish we had more money and more members, the strength of the auxiliary, to me, is the special love our members have for it.

Ruth Singler. As I think about the history of AMVETS and all that has been accomplished, it makes me very proud to have been a part of it by serving as national president. Many things were accomplished in that year; here are a few.

In September, Philippine President Ferdinand Marcos and his wife visited this country and I had the pleasure of representing the auxiliary. A few months later, I was in Washington, D.C., to help celebrate the "Welcome Home to Vietnam Veterans." National Commander Robert Martin and I were privileged to be a part of the reviewing stand for the parade honoring these veterans.

On Veterans Day, I was able to meet President Ronald Reagan during a visit to the White House. Afterwards, we were escorted on special buses to Arlington National Cemetery, where the ceremonies were held.

Then on December 5, I participated in the rededication of the carillon on the *Arizona* Memorial at Pearl Harbor. The national commander, several members of AMVETS and the auxiliary, together with military personnel stationed in and around Pearl Harbor took part in the ceremony.

There is no way of expressing what one feels when you realize you are actually standing over the battleship *Arizona* and that 1,102 crewmen are still interred there. This realization is brought quickly to mind when you walk to the back of the memorial and see the marble wall with the names of all those servicemen. It makes me even more proud to be a part of its history since AMVETS donated the wall.

In February, I took part in the "AMVETS Return to the Philippines" program. Thanks to Commander Martin, I was the first national president invited to go on this trip. We followed this in April with a visit to Taiwan to attend the convention of the Vocational Assistance Commission for Retired Servicemen (VACRS).

The theme for my year as national president was "Service That Shines" and as I look back over the years, it was certainly a year that did shine.

National Presidents

Agnes P. Kolano. "Helping Others Coast to Coast" was my theme as national president 1983-84.

The John Tracy Clinic for Pre-school Deaf Children was one of my pet projects promoted heavily throughout the states. Commander Wilbraham and I worked together on promoting the Pearl S. Buck Foundation Program for Amerasian children. While on tour in the Philippines, we visited their headquarters and presented gifts to 19 children. The tour will always be a treasured memory.

One of the most outstanding events I ever experienced was our Silver Helmet Banquet. There, I had the privilege of presenting Congressman John S. McCain with the Auxiliary Humanitarian Award.

A very emotional moment that occurred during my reign was when I extended greetings at the rededication of the U.S.S. *Arizona* Memorial Wall in Hawaii. The event was so moving and I will never forget it.

This was a year I started the ball rolling on relocating Auxiliary National Headquarters from Old Orchard Beach, Maine, to Lanham, Md. At the NEC meeting in 1984, the resolution was accepted and we moved the auxiliary headquarters to Maryland.

Indeed, 1983-84 was a memorable year of hard work, time and devotion and I shall treasure each and every day of it.

Betty M. Wineland. The year of 1984-85 was a new beginning. It was also a year of transition and dramatic change. Through the efforts of our Move and Search Committee and the continued cooperation of AMVETS National Headquarters, we moved the auxiliary headquarters from Maine to Lanham, Md.

During my term, we accepted challenges with the help of dedicated members, who were willing to strive to expand our objectives and growth even further, and believed in taking risks. It has paid off! Within only 9 short years (since 1984), the percentage of growth in volunteer service increased—not only to the veteran, his wife and children, or the patients in the veterans hospitals, but to the communities, nursing homes and programs supported by our auxiliary members. Membership has reached a new high—far above any predictions, with one state having more than 6,500 members.

During this year, AMVETS National Service Foundation presented the auxiliary with a grant of $2,000 to establish a pilot school of instructions program. This enabled us to provide, with the assistance of three instructors, valuable information concerning the auxiliary's programs and procedures.

It was an honor to present the auxiliary's Humanitarian Award to Bill Kurtis of CBS News for his work in television journalism on Agent Orange and the plight of Amerasian children. It was also an honor to serve as a judge on the jury at Freedoms Foundation to select persons worthy of receiving the foundation's prestigious George Washington Medal of Honor and other awards.

I was able to travel to 20 states, including Alaska and Oregon; visit the Philippine Islands for the 40th Anniversary of the liberation of Manila; and dedicate a carillon in the American Cemetery in Manila. As a guest of the RSEA Company in Taipei, Taiwan, we saw firsthand its facilities that housed retiring servicemen. Dignitaries of the Vocational Assistance Commission for Retired Servicemen also gave us an impressive tour.

On our second visit to Taipei, we represented the United States at the VACRS' International Convention that included representatives from Africa, Sweden and other European countries.

During my year, I was made to feel like a citizen of several states; resolutions were presented by the House of Representatives honoring me and I was interviewed by the media. But the people were the most important part of my term—both AMVETS and auxiliary members. These are faces I remember, not just as president, but in my 40 years as an AMVET Auxiliary member.

Mary S. Barrow. During my term as national president of the AMVETS Auxiliary, I have spoken of the Spirit of '86—a spirit of service to our God, our nation, and our neighbors. I have tried to convey this spirit during my travels while in office, and I have felt the spirit being returned to me by our energetic and enthusiastic volunteers everywhere. —*1986 Convention Journal*

Sylvia Lipowski. When I assumed the position as national president of the AMVETS Auxiliary, I set many goals. One of them was to create a "good climate" for all members and to make the AMVETS and auxiliary experience a pleasurable one.

Choosing the theme "Service with Heart," I worked on encouraging volunteerism in all aspects of AMVETS and auxiliary programs. As a former teacher, working on programs with children and projects for our veterans was closest to my heart.

Through my travels and personal contacts with members, I promoted programs such as the John Tracy Clinic, Abused Children, Amerasian Children, Special Olympics, scholarships, and patriotism among youth through the Americanism poster and essay contests and Freedoms Foundation.

I had the honor of representing the auxiliary at the national VAVS advisory meetings, at the USO and at the Pearl S. Buck Foundation. I received the Legion of Honor Medal from the Chapel of Four Chaplains and established an annual Americanism Seminar at Freedoms Foundation.

Aside from visiting posts, auxiliaries and VA medical centers across the country, I visited Pearl Harbor, Arlington National Cemetery and the Vietnam Veterans Memorial; I felt a great sense of remembrance and loss while looking at the Wall.

My husband Joe and I visited Normandy, France, to attend a carillon dedication at the U.S. National Cemetery. As I stood on the beach where my own brother had landed on D-Day, I thought about how lucky I was that he came home safe.

Traveling across America, I felt the warmth and hospitality that is a part of our organization. Someone said the memories of a man in his old age are the deeds of a man in his prime. These special memories are forever etched in my mind.

Dorothy J. Stoddard. Among her goals for the AMVETS Auxiliary is to see that the organization reaches its tremendous potential. She feels strongly that greater participation in legislative action affecting veterans is a must. Also, she is convinced that continued support and improvement of our programs will make the auxiliary stronger and will set an example for future leaders to follow. —*Auxiliary Archives*

National Presidents

Betty J. Leisure. For her term, Betty chose the theme "Together We Can," which became a trademark of her personality. She emphasized the need for teamwork on all levels of the auxiliary "to better serve the veteran and our communities." During her term as first vice president, auxiliary membership had increased 13 percent.

—Auxiliary Archives

DECEASED

Jean Baxter. How proud I am of all the success we have achieved and the growth we have accomplished . . . . Our membership is steadily increasing and so are the total hours spent working on our Americanism, community service and child-welfare programs. Our scholarship program is a great success . . . . While we were disappointed that Abigail "Dear Abby" Van Buren was unable to attend the Silver Helmet Banquet . . . to receive the Auxiliary Humanitarian Award, I had the opportunity to talk with Kevin Dobson and James Brady, both of whom give freely of themselves to further the lives of their fellow man. *—The National AMVET*

Nita I. Cornell. As I reflect on my year of service, among the many instances that come to mind is playing an active role in the Youth Conference at Freedoms Foundation. The foundation itself was very important to me. At the annual seminar sponsored by the AMVETS Auxiliary, the 5-year commitment by all auxiliaries and states to raise $54,000 to renovate the Franklin Building was established and our first payment of $8,000 made.

To visit auxiliaries and experience their "Working Together" to make a difference in their communities and states was exhilarating.

I'm thankful that "Desert Watch" progressed into a short "Desert Storm" and onto "Desert Calm" during my year. The unity displayed by people in support of our troops was very gratifying.

If I had to choose an outstanding reflection, I would have to say my visit to Guard Post Oullette, located at the uppermost northern corner of South Korea. To realize troops are there, willing to serve, is a unique experience I will truly never forget.

To have served as national president of the AMVETS Auxiliary following 30 years as a member is something I will long remember with fond memories.

Dorothy R. Bull. The main highlights of my year were meeting all the beautiful auxiliary and AMVETS members as I traveled this nation from east to west and north to south. Their dedication to the work we do was astounding.

My trip to Hawaii to commemorate the 50th Anniversary of the bombing of Pearl Harbor is something I'll never forget. When I visited the U.S.S *Arizona* and realized there were still men entombed there, I felt emotions that could not be described. It was also my privilege to be a part of those ceremonies dedicating the U.S.S. *Arizona* Room at national headquarters.

As the year moved along, I attended the Youth Seminar at Freedoms Foundation for the first time. After that trip, I realized the importance of this program.

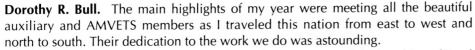

Another vital program is Paws With A Cause. The largest donation ever made to "Paws" was given this year by the national auxiliary.

My trip to Korea and Taiwan was another interesting and enlightening trip. I met many interesting people and had the opportunity to experience their history.

New auxiliaries were organized in Oklahoma, Alaska and West Virginia, which increased membership.

Anne Hall, auxiliary convention chairperson, and Gloria Jasinski, co-chairman, did a beautiful job on the convention held in Orlando, Fla. The convention was unique in that we held a resource fair instead of workshops. The convention was dedicated to the past national commanders and past national presidents.

It was a memorable year. I will never forget it and all the auxiliary members, AMVETS and veterans that I was privileged to meet.

Betty S. Lawson. I can honestly say this has been a most enjoyable and interesting year that I shall never forget. The courtesies extended to me during my visits, renewing old friendships, and making new friends made it outstanding . . . . As we assess our year, it is with pride that we report increases in our services, volunteers and membership. By "Working Together for a Greater America," we have made a significant contribution toward making our communities, our states and our nation better for all . . . . It has been an honor and a privilege to have served as your national president and I will always be available to assist AMVETS and the AMVETS Auxiliary.

—THE NATIONAL AMVET

Barbara S. Hinsley. Every trip I took and every member I met was very important to me. The local members are the ones who do the work, and they may never see a national president or any national officer. It was a pleasure for me to meet each one of them. The hospitality that was shown to me in every post I visited was outstanding. The only problem was that they feed you too much.

Having met some of the famous people that I have also means a lot to me. Roy Rogers, Efram Zimbalist, Hugh O'Brien, Jesse Brown, President and Mrs. Clinton are just a few of them. When I think of these people, I remember all the places I have been—most of which would never have been possible if I had not been elected your president. That is why I have always tried to represent you and the organization to the best of my ability.

One trip I'll always treasure was the one to the Far East. Enroute, we stopped in Hawaii, and Commander Hearon and I laid wreaths at the U.S.S. *Arizona* Memorial and the National Cemetery of the Pacific. Then we left for Taiwan, where we were the guests of the Vocational Assistance Commission for Retired Servicemen. I will never forget the places we visited and things we saw there, including a veterans home and hospital. Several days after returning home, I left for Normandy. It was the opportunity of a lifetime—not just to see all the programs that were planned or to be involved in some of the activities, but to be there with the veterans of D-Day. I talked with some of them and heard others talking to each other. It was the most heart-rendering experience I have ever been a part of.

Ed Note: *A number of auxiliary programs were not included in the reflections of various national presidents. During the term of Kathryn Snyder, for example, the Hospital Program was established, followed by the Serve Our Servicemen Program under Evelyn Lauritson. In 1963, a program was started under Leah Monasterio to raise funds to furnish two dormitory rooms at Freedoms Foundation. Three years later, this project was completed when Jewel Fifielski presented the foundation with a check for $7,500. The National Scholarship Program was adopted under Ellen Bogatay, with the first rehabilitation scholarship being awarded during the term of Rita Potvin. Finally, the Adopt-a-Room Program, begun in 1990 under Nita Cornell (page 99), was completed in 1993 during the term of Barbara Hinsley.*

Credits

4, 6, 8, 10 (top), *18, 20* (right), *21* (top), *43* (middle), *47* (bottom right and left), *48, 64*–Brendan Mattingly; *9, 38* (top right)–U.S. Navy; *10* (bottom)–Bill Mauldin, reprinted by permission of the author and the Watkins/Loomis Agency; *11, 14, 15* (left and bottom), *27* (bottom left), *51* (bottom left), *53, 54* (top left)–White House; *12*–Del Ankers; *15*–Sgt. John Babyak, Jr. (U.S. Marine Corps); *16*–Feiler Studio; *19* (bottom)–International News Photos; *20* (top left), *63* (top middle)–Greg Floberg; *21* (bottom), *24* (bottom), *30* (bottom), *33* (top left), *42, 43* (top), *52* (bottom), *63* (middle)–Tom Kozar; *22* (bottom), *27* (bottom right)–Charles Rumel; *29, 30* (middle), *32* (middle and bottom), *43* (bottom)–Day Walters; *31* (middle), *32* (right), *39* (top right), *59* (bottom)–Capitol Photo Service Inc.; *34* (top right), *36, 62* (bottom right)–Danny Devine; *41* (top left)–David Yamada, *Honolulu Advertiser*, (bottom)–Camera Hawaii; *45*–Rick Shannon; *50* (top)–VA Photo, (bottom)–Dick Flanagan; *51* (top)–©1986 by Nick Cerulli; (bottom right)–*Providence Journal-Bulletin*; *54* (except top left), *55*–copyrighted by the White House Historical Association, photographs by the National Geographic Society; *50* (left)–Ham Fisher, ©1949, by the McNaught Syndicate; *57* (bottom right)–Harris & Ewing; *59* (top left)–copyrighted by the *Fresno Bee*; *60* (bottom left)–copyrighted by Pontificia Fotografi; *63* (bottom)–North Carolina Post 920.

Acknowledgments

I wish to express my gratitude to the members of the AMVETS 50th Anniversary Committee—PNC Dante Spagnolo, chairman; Al Bartel; PNC Harold Berc; PNC Vaughn Brown, Sr.; PNP Toni Gomulinski; PNC Ralph Hall; Frank Huray; Arthur Klingel, Jr.; PNP Betty Lawson; PNP Sylvia Lipowski; PNC Robert Martin; PNC Marshall Miller and Kenneth Wolford—for their support and assistance during the time this history was being compiled. I am also grateful to Albert Geremia and those past national commanders and past national presidents who answered my requests for information. The input and materials they furnished were invaluable.

I owe a special thank-you to my assistant, Tonya Swann, for her help in editing and proofing, and the many phone calls she made to procure artwork and verify information. I similarly appreciate the research assistance provided by our college intern, LaSandra Purnell from Bowie State University.

I would be remiss if I didn't acknowledge the help I received from Richard Maurey, Lois Raimond and Karen Cleek of Graphica, and Lottie Ketcham and Robert Klem of Stephenson Printing. Their counsel, patience and willingness to do whatever was necessary to meet the deadlines imposed by this project certainly made my job easier.

Finally, to my wife Ellen who was a source of constant encouragement to me during the many hours spent working on the book, I am forever indebted.
                                                        —*Dick Flanagan, July 1994*

National
Charter Members

Arizona
Raymond D. Beving
Joseph F. Biondo
Russell O. Bollman
Lloyd P. Bourn
Louie Davidson
Rocco Dichristofano
Phyllis J. Ehrman
James Lambert
Joseph J. Lesk
Eugene I. Michal
Merlin Mueller
Thomas D. Nesmith
Raymond M. Sayre
George Schack
Kenneth E. Steege
Donnell H. Stoltzfus
Karl R. Thiel
Dorothy Wooddell
Casimir Worso

Arkansas
Dansby A. Council
Joseph F. Piaskowy
Jack N. Sowder

California
John H. Ackerman
Ronald Almond
Ralph R. Anderson, Jr.
Howard E. Austin
Louis L. Baron
Charles W. Begg
Edward W. Branum
Mary W. Branum
Marold W. Brown
Raymond K. Cornick
Vincent Cruz
John O. Davies
Edward M. Furner
Betty Gollnick
Alicia S. Grant
Ray E. Guttormson
Leroy F. Hasson
David Hogan, Jr.
J. L. Jolley
John O. Jonassen
Duarward A. Jones
James J. Kehoe
Don E. Kinnison
John E. Lackey
Richard Marquis
James C. Moody
Joy Nishimoto
Edgar D. Powell
William F. Riggs

Florence A. Ring
Joseph R. Rivas, Sr.
Faith D. Rothburn
Nathaniel S. Ruvell
Manuel Toledo
Daniel J. Valdez
Jackie M. Voelkl
Frederick R. Wesbey
William B. Whitman

Connecticut
Alfred Marzullo
Earl Pleu
Louis V. Valente
William M. Welch

District of Columbia
Harry M. DeWitt
Jim G. Lucas

Florida
Eldridge Adams
Stewart G. Allen
Robert J. Andrews
Florian J. Banasik
Clyde Blanton
Louis W. Brunnet
John B. Cahill
C. E. Clauson
Norman E. Clock
Lawrence J. Curran
William C. Dahlberg
Benjamin A. DeLucci
Richard H. Dewey
Jerry Eckert
Frederick L. Falk
John J. Fitzner
Clinton Gamble
Dale R. Gidel
Joseph R. Gill
John G. Hatz
John M. Hengely
George Holgash
Mabel E. Hunter
Charles Hyatt
Ernest Kahn
John A. Kallanj
Harold A. Keats
Leonard Kogut
Walter S. Kolankowski, Jr.
Peter Kramer
Nick R. Lippucci
Antonio Maberino
Wilton B. Mackall
Chris March
Ted March

Angelina F. Mazzarelli
James J. McLimans
Charles E. Means
Jeremiah Morales
Donald A. Norton
Nick Panchula
Richard B. Paul
G. H. Peace
Felix A. Rammel
Arthur H. Rude
Frank J. Scarane
Walter Skowron
Leonard A. Skubal
John S. Spain
Wanda M. Stapela
Arnold A. Steinke
Patrick J. Wallace
John A. Washburn
Raymond Weber
Ivan M. Wheeler
Edward F. Whitley
Lynn A. Wiley

Georgia
George W. Brown
Henry E. Conner
J. S. Crespi
Daryl Dunckel
C. J. Eller
George L. Floyd
Ray Gillad
Ralph Howington
Ernest E. Huddleston
Darrell Long
James Martin
C. B. McIntyre
Algernon F. Meeks
Duette Morre
George Morris
Billy R. Patterson
Don E. Smith

Idaho
Carl H. Anderson
Fred A. Illian

Illinois
Walter J. Abrant
George Abruzino
James R. Adams
Lloyd E. Adolphson
George Albee
Harry J. Allenbrand
Casimir J. Alwin
George F. Andersen
G. Carolyn Anderson

Alex Andreoni
Albert C. Andrulis
Joseph A. Angelo
Dorothy Ashford
Henry J. Augustyn
Walter E. Babiarz
Robert P. Bacon
Ralph Baker
Sam Barbera
Paul W. Barker
Harry E. Barnes
Edward M. Bartecki
William J. Bauer
Kenneth L. Baxter
William O. Bay
Lyle E. Bayler
George T. Becker
Willard F. Beckstine
Alfred E. Berbig
Harold T. Berc
Ellsworth O. Beyer
John E. Biegus
Alphonse S. Bielawski
Arthur J. Biggins
John F. Biggio
Kenneth Biggs
Gordon J. Bigsby
Floyd D. Birkey
Marvin A. Birkey
Ralph H. Blair
Laverne H. Bloom
Bernard Edward Bolotoff
Myron A. Bradford
Edward M. Brennan
John A. Broderick
Faye R. Brown
William J. Bryant
Robert A. Buchanan
Marvin Buetsch
Joseph F. Bukovsky
James V. Buletty
Patrick A. Burke
Stanley J. Burkot
George J. Burns, Sr.
Michael J. Byrne, Jr.
Damian E. Caffrey, Sr.
Lyle R. Cagle
Arthur M. Carlson
Benjamin Charlier
Edwin B. Charzempa
William M. Choronzak
Charles F. Christensen
E. C. Churchill, Jr.
Stanley G. Ciesla
Edwin R. Cisne
Bernard T. Clark

Wilbert W. Claus
Joseph E. Cleary
Granville H. Coburn
D. Arthur Connelly
Ira D. Cravens
William D. Cribbens
Edward D. Crowcroft
Raymond Cummings
Dwayne A. Daniels
Rex L. Davis
Norman Denzinger
Lawrence Deruy
Edward A. Doyle
Joseph W. Draus
Richard Dykes
Carl W. Ehlen
Ralph J. Einhorn
Lorin A. Ellsworth
Edward W. Ennis
Egron G. Erickson
James J. Farmer
Peter M. Fausone
John P. Feely
Gerald W. Forsyth
Theodore Friedman
A. J. Frymark
Andrew Fryntzko
Robert A. Galarowicz
Barbara Gale
Joseph F. Galica
Leon Gavin
Vernon Gehlbach
Sam J. George
Samuel Gnoffo
John Gockel
Tony E. Gockel
Harry J. Goetz
Walter T. Goldsworthy
Robert W. Grawley
Raymond T. Gundlock
Charles V. Hall
Rodney J. Hall
Robert E. Hanley
M. D. Haun
James E. Hayes
Walter T. Hayes
Frank A. Heckman
Raymond M. Hederman
Robert L. Helsley
J. Jud Henninger
Glade Hewerdine
William H. Hillmer
Robert E. Hines
Anthony F. Hlousek
Clair A. Hogan
Donald F. Hogan

G. William Horsley
Mitchell T. Hossa
Bernard R. Houdek
John Hribar
Owen Hudson
Paul E. Huska
Orin C. Hutchcraft
Victor D. Hyatt
Frank P. Ingraffa
Lawrence Irving
Vernon F. Jereb
Herbert C. Jiranek
Erwin F. Johnson
George E. Johnson
Warner E. Johnson
Thomas R. Kelly
William T. Kelly
Walter B. Kichura
Maurice J. Korengold
Chester C. Kosinski
Eugene J. Koziol
Edward A. Krones
Leonard S. Kukowinski
Stanley Kulak
Joseph E. Kwiatt
Martin A. Lammer
Jack Lampert
Theron H. Lane
Harold G. LeRoy
Raymond Leesman
Raymond E. Loeber
Donald G. Long
Edward R. Lorek
Michael F. Lynch
Frank J. Majka
Rex Manninger
Alexander Mashko
Henry J. Matick
Rubin Matin
Joseph P. Matray
Clarence Mazan
Charles M. McArty, Sr.
Jack McFetridge
Thomas F. McKenna
Edward T. McKiernan
Orville C. McLendon
Robert B. McNeil
Paul J. Melahn, Jr.
Walter F. Michna
William J. Migon
Catherine C. Moore
Emmett J. Mulloy
John P. Myers
Albert Nehf
Marietta Neil
Harold T. Neiman

Kenneth R. Nelson
Royal J. Nichols
Henry F. Nowak
George W. Nye
John J. O'Connell
Kenneth E. Olson
Henry E. Ostapa
Austin Owens
Joseph W. Ozgowicz
Benny Pabisinski
Elroy Paschedag, Jr.
Edgar A. Patrick
Stanley F. Pawlikowski
Fred A. Pehrkon
Carl Peterson
Charles E. Pickens
Russell H. Pickens
Charles C. Pickerill
Edward J. Pienczak
Clarence H. Plum
William Port
Charles Powell
Arlie C. Proctor
Frederick F. Pruyn
Ted Przybylo
Stanley S. Rakowski
Daniel J. Ralph
John C. Randell
David J. Reardon
Richard A. Reece
Cyril Riess
Ralph Rose, Jr.
Ernest D. Rosenbery
Thomas M. Rotella
Harry Roush
James J. Ryan
Walter J. Sadlowski
Edward A. Samborski
Charles Sammons
John J. Schaaf
Francis W. Schnell
Jack M. Schulman
Lawrence W. Seborg
John F. Sexton
Michael Robert Sherrock
John A. Skreko
Matthew W. Slowik
Harry P. Sommerlad
Floyd Spaenhower
Arnold E. Spangler
Joseph Sprajcar
George J. Staab, Jr.
Vincent E. Staab
John J. Stepek
Herman Steward
Leonard J. Strojny

Clarence Sullivan
Daniel F. Sullivan
John F. Sweeney
Elmer S. Swiatkowski
Lincoln S. Tamraz
Allan R. Tanner
Clifford E. Taylor
Irvin R. Tchon
Earl W. Thomas
Carl G. H. Tofte
Frank H. Trisch
Rosalie V. G. Vance
Theodore Visin
Philip H. Vision
Phil Vock
Larry J. Vonic
Russell R. Walker
Robert K. Warszynski
Albert E. Wharmby
Charles M. Whitmore, Jr.
Billy B. Wiese
Carl E. Wilkey
Charles R. Wilkins, Jr.
Carl W. Yager, Jr.
Jose F. Ybarra
Ben M. Yokley
Stanley E. Zeglicz
Joseph F. T. Zemerowski
Dragutin Zuzuly

Indiana
Anthony L. Adomaitis
Edmund G. Barnes
Richard Barnes
Earl Groll
Walter H. Hagerdon
James R. Johnson
George T. Phelan
W. M. Stepnakowski
Loren E. Sturgeon
Wayne E. Weisheit

Iowa
Arnold F. Andersen
Clarence Anderson
Ward Anderson
Russell I. Aries
George W. Baker
Mabel S. Beggs
Edward Bixby
DeLane W. Brechwald
James L. Brown
Edward H. Bryden
Ray Busching
Calvin U. Carlson
Lawrence Cratty

National
Charter Members

Harry Curry
Robert Davis
James W. Duschen
Harold L. Ellerbach
Hubert Ellison
Robert Fresner
Foster Funk
Robert Geick
Robert George
Leonard Gibson
Irwin F. Giss
Irwin Goos
Harold E. Hansen
Kenneth Harms
Ernie Harnisch
William L. Harvey
Cal Haub
Paul Hoogheem
George R. Huff
Harold L. Jensen
James F. Johnson
Marshall W. Judd
Donald Kerr
Vernon Kerr
Eugene Kliebenstein
Frank Klumpar
Maurice Kuhr
James C. Lyon
William V. MacKenzie
Glen W. Mahmens
R. J. McFarland
Floyd Messerly
Melvin E. Meyerhoff
Carl Mikes
Harrison Moench
Ted Moldenhauer
Kenneth H. Nelson
John Pasko
Hugh F. Patterson
Albert D. Petersen
Wayne C. Philp
E. L. Reinhard
Bernard H. Reynolds
Walter S. Rieck
Ervin Ruff
W. A. Sandburg
Irving Schierholz
Albert Schirm
Ralph Schmadeke
Russell M. Seymour
Robert Snell
James E. Storjohann
Keith Stover
Royce A. Strayer
Wendel Stuart
Marvin D. Stumpf

Truman D. Sweet
Gene Taylor
Donald L. Triplett
Alvin Troll
Darwin Vint
Earl J. Vogel
Donald E. Walter
Lester C. Wilson
Kenneth Zierke

Kansas
Lee R. Higgins

Kentucky
William M. Bayer
Donald H. Drayer
William F. Eversole
Charles G. Kelty

Louisiana
Laure Adoue
Frank V. Anzalone
Vincent J. Anzalone
Marion A. Cangelosi
Joseph D. Deblieux
Anthony J. DeFrances
Tom Gillen, Jr.
Joseph C. Hebert
Tom S. Hicks
Alma S. Jolly
James Kinman
Russell Long
Lester Marden, Jr.
Robert Martin
Bert J. Ourso
Ory G. Poret
Marshall M. Pratt, Jr.
Grace Prestridge
J. R. Raymond
Raymond Rockhold
F. J. Rouyer
Joseph W. Sanders
Hester T. Thompson
Cleve A. Willett
Harold Young

Maine
Wayne A. Bazemore
Alvin Brandt
James H. Cram
Clifton E. Currier
James Dufour
Joseph Gregoire
Willie Grover
Norman J. Marquis
Reginald McBean, Jr.

Maurice W. Moreau
Ceylon Putnam
Clifford W. Ranger
Steve Waite
Jerry Woods

Maryland
George J. Allen
Robert K. Grove
Edward C. Hedges
J. H. Keller
Horace Z. Opel
Charles C. Pearl
David Pogoloff
Lester E. Spear
Ellis H. Stroup
John C. Ward
Frank Wolin

Massachusetts
Steve E. Adams
Kenneth A. Arris
Liborio Bevilacqua
Robert L. Brennan
John J. Canty, Jr.
Oldemiro Canto
George M. Carson
George L. Cawley
Leo F. Cebula
Joseph S. Chupal
Lucille G. Clark
Charles E. Couch
William P. Dimeo
Alfred J. Falkland
Charles T. Fox
Joseph L. Francis
Robert G. Fuller
Benedict Gudinas
Robert J. Guertin
Calvin H. Gurney
James B. Hennessey
Albert E. Houde, Sr.
Camille Houde
Forrest Howard
John T. Kerrigan
George J. Leurini
Oscar F. London
Frances E. Mason
George H. McCue
George V. Medeiros
Vartan Mekalian
Eino O. Parker
Phyllis M. Pierce
Edward Sands
John A. Sands
Harold A. Smith

Albert Sorrentino
Ernest G. Spaulding
Kenneth P. Spraque
Frank P. Talarico
Edward A. Terry
Leo G. Tessier
Leo P. Thibault
Peter P. Urban
David N. Warner
Daniel J. Wholley

Michigan
Leo J. Arickx
Richard D. Bourassa
John T. Carroll
Stanley Cetnor
Harold J. Clark
Florence Cozma
John Cozma
Michael D. Cyrbok
Helga A. Dow
Leonard Duda
John Favenyes
Amy M. Feluk
Wayne W. Ferris
Cornell Foltuz
Stanley Fredericks
Joseph Glowacz
William H. Higgins
Carl Hillard
Robert K. Hosley
Robert Johnson
Vernelle Johnson
Eugene Kacanowski
Louis V. Koveri
Anthony Krukowski
Walter Kushnir
Raymond J. Land
Benny LaRocca
Ted Liwienski
Joseph A. Meagher
George Mlinaz
Leo Moga
Carl Mosberg
Leonard Nelson
Walter C. Oginski
John Pawelek
Norman J. Petersen
Martin Pytel
Arthur Ring
Julian Rutherford
Michael Ryback
James Schaefer
James G. Sebel
Edward Setlock
Ted Smolen

Tom Sparks
Edward Sternicki
John M. Sternicki, Jr.
Walter Sternicki
Leroy Taylor
Norman Thieda
Frank Traka
M. E. Van Brocklin
William C. Weed
William B. Wilford
Frank Ziska
Joseph A. Zuker

Missouri
Elwood E. Adams
Ronald Ambrose
Charles Benson, Jr.
Irving C. Erhardt
Erwin Gummels
Alvin W. Knackstedt
Harry Lay
James Parkin
Clifford V. Potts
Walter R. Reeve
Arthur F. Schmitz
Hardy J. Smith

Nevada
George J. Kolodziejski
Albert J. Leoni
Alfonse Tombrello

New Hampshire
David F. Gagnon
James Gibson

New Jersey
Anthony W. Andriola
George Biello, Sr.
William A. Boyle
Harry W. Chenoweth
James A. Delissio
Jack Franzi
Frank Geusic
Leo J. Giangrande
Leonard E. Goralczyk
Frank Horner
Harold F. Laudien
Gerald Longo
Michael V. Marotti
Carmen Mazza
Fred J. Moser
Julius R. Pollatschek
Stanley J. Reczka
Russell Rickards
Nelson W. Rummel

Peter J. Seman
George T. Vosseler

New York
Roger Avery
William Belinson
Wallace Bolewski
Anthony Cellio
Dominic Cellio
Eugene Corcoran
Walter Dams
Sarah K. Early
Matt A. Gajewski
Richard Gardner
Joseph Greco, Jr.
Knute L. Grytebust
William H. Hackradt
Edward Hauptmann
Arthur Higgins
Joseph Jastry
Fred L. Knapczyk
Carmine LaMagna
Pat Lupinacci
Richard Magierski
Louis E. Matuszewski
Alfred Paggiotta
Angelo Perry
John Ranellone
Benjamin Rieck
George Sarkis
Vincent A. Strempski
Rudolph J. Walter
Kenneth Weber
Harold F. Welker

North Carolina
Bruce D. Davis
Lloyd E. Helgeland
Paul R. Hester
Jay C. Kivett
Calvin Morris
Bryce Murdock
Edward Powell
V. G. Price, Jr.
Bill Revelle
Darrell Skipper
Allen L. Smith
Dante E. Spagnolo
Lloyd A. Whitworth

Ohio
Ivan E. Amerine
Delton Baker
Ernest Banzy
Paul J. Bartak
Raphael Bartholow

Joseph Beck
Harold G. Billhorn
Joseph Bozzacco
John Carew
Ralph F. Claflin
James Conn
Fred Crawford
James L. Cummings
Frank Czyzynski
Norman Denzinger
Louis G. Doerr
Robert Ewing
Norman B. Fink
James R. Ford
Stanton Fox
Alvin Frazier
Harold Fulmer
E. G. Galehouse
Robert J. Gizzo
Glenn Goerl
Robert N. Goldney
Joseph A. Grigoli
Edward J. Grill
Abe E. Haas
Walter H. Hagerdon
Norman S. Hakes
Jerry G. Hanacek
Frank Heitz
Michael Hollop
George Ilchak
Donald Janda
Frank S. Kalicky
Bernard J. Kawalski
Melvin C. Koch
Robert R. Koepke
Robert W. Lewis
Albert A. Lindquist
John J. Lolla
William Mackiewicz
Wayne Markley
Ernest C. Marshall
James E. McGinnis
Kenneth G. Miller
Paul F. Miller
Robert C. Miller
Fred J. Milligan
Richard Modzell
Richard Nixon
Robert J. O'Neil
Mike Oana
Norman W. Pallotta
Richard Paysor
Francis Picarski
Don Quinn
Harry F. Reilman
Joe Repas

Richard J. Rinebolt
Albert H. Robey
Stuart J. Satullo
Clement E. Schirtzinger
Maurice Sechler
Rix Seibert
Floyd E. Shaum
Alvin Simmer
Frank Sislowski
Thomas Slattery
John Strange
James Suchy
Laurence Sutphen
Gus Tarian
Paul E. Truman
William J. Vida
Ernest H. Walters
Andrew Wansack
William M. Ward
William R. Warden
Clifford W. Waters
Charles Weinle
Wilma Williams
James W. Willman
Edward Wisneski
Harold Ziegler
James Zoubek
Andrew C. Zufall

Oklahoma
Kenneth Miller
Ray Sawyer

Pennsylvania
Art Abbotts
John Q. Adams
Frank K. Alexander
Edward Alinsky
Leonard Ambrose
Paul C. Amspacher
Frank J. Antinozzi
Joseph J. Antosz
Andrew A. Augustine
Stanley Babiak
Adam Balkiewicz
Andrew A. Baloga
Walter E. Bantom, Jr.
Ray Barkley
Thomas Barry
John Batche
Martin A. Bebar
Carroll D. Bechtel, Jr.
Robert Bechtel
Carl W. Bennett
Oscar J. Bennett
Frank A. Bialas

National Charter Members

Carmen Biello
Martin J. Bitschley, Jr.
George H. Bixler
Tony Blazauski
Fred J. Bogatay
John Bokrosh
John J. Boles
John Bolkovac
Mark F. Bolkovac
Edward F. Bomba
Guy A. Bowe, Jr.
Herbert G. Breitinger
Frank J. Briggins
Albert Britz
Roy A. Brown
Vaughn L. Brown, Sr.
Henry Brunett, Jr.
Clyde J. Brunnet
Lincoln K. P. Buchanan
Roman Bydlon
Ralph Calig
Michael T. Carduff
Charles D. Carl
William G. Cavalcante
Joseph Cerceo
Leonard Chaikowsky
Frank Cherepko
John Cherepko
Albert Chernisky
Joseph Chobany, Jr.
Andrew Ciokota
Michael J. Corodi
William H. Craig
James C. Cunningham
William J. Daehnke
Pietro Dallo
W. Farel Davidheiser
Gaetano DeRitis
Irvin R. Dehaven
Joseph Demora
Roy M. Dettinger
Donald Dickey
Edward T. Ditzler
William B. Dornsife
John A. Durany
Norman S. Eckert
Albert Eleoterio
Anthony Eleoterio
Michael Enedy, Sr.
Harold D. Eschbach
Robert D. Evans
David Fessler
Ernest K. Flesher
Charles J. Foanio
James A. Foanio
Joseph E. Fodor

Richard S. Frain
Gino Frescura
Gerald L. Frock
William G. Gale
Philip Gatto
Frank W. Gaudlip
Joseph T. Geusic
Joseph D. Giannini
John Giordano
Robert R. Gorchik
Joseph Gozdzasek
John B. Graffius
William Greenaway
Joseph Harris
Michael Havrilla
Steve Havrilla
Harry G. Hayes
Joseph J. Hebda
George Hedricks Jr.
Robert Heidenfelder
Ward M. Heiser
Carl Heller
Aldus J. Herr
Stanley Homce
Adam S. Horowski
Charles J. Horowski
Stanley J. Horowski
David Howard
Michael Hrichision
James F. Hubbert, Sr.
John A. Humbert
Luther Humbert
Edself Hurwitz
Richard P. Jacoby
Olive H. D. Johnson
Edward W. Jones
Eldred B. Jones
William Kambic
Burd J. Kaufman
Fred Klementovic
Harry Klink
William Knight
Alex Koliga
Paul J. Korche
Stanley J. Kozloski
Ernest Krammes
Ernest L. Krause
Leo L. Krause
Robert F. Krause
Michael Kravitski
Casimir J. Krawinski
John B. Krebs
Edgar L. Krug
John J. Kucey
Joseph Kuzeck
Joseph Lapos

Joseph Lees
Glenn R. Lesher
John Letcavage
Jack J. Lewis
Peter J. Ligenza
Kenneth W. Logan
Nicholas Lombard
George W. Long
Howard R. Long
Robert N. Long
John Lutzkanin
Bernard Mack
Rudy Manak
Joseph S. Manko
Louis A. Marsalko
John B. Mayers
Harold M. McCamley
Michael Melnic
Guy S. Mengel
Esli S. Meyers, Jr.
Sol J. Michael
Edward J. Michalowski
Stanley B. Mikulski
Anthony F. Miller
Paul A. Miller, Jr.
John P. Modrick
Frank M. Modrick
Charles S. Mohn
Francis R. Monci
Frank P. Mutch
Charles C. Nalbach
Michael J. Namovage
Michael N. Nazak
Joseph E. Olexy
John Orach
Zeno Orsingher
William Partridge
Harry Pastovich
Irvin E. Peiffer
Paul R. Peiffer
Russell L. Peiffer
William A. Peiffer
N. Perbetsky, Jr.
Al Perlinsky
Edward R. Persin
Manfred J. Peterson
Roman Petrusky
Allen Phillips
William Pinkerton
George Pohlod
Joseph Pohopin
Michael Pohopin
John Pokryzwa
Edward Pollock
David W. Pry
Eugene F. Rabenstine

Paul Racko
Charles S. Ranker
Michael Raptosh
Allen J. Reed
George O. Rhoads, Sr.
Donald L. Richmond
Donald M. Richter
J. Harold Rife
Al Robel
Francis Roberts
Marco A. Rodriguez
Charles L. Roeder
Joseph Rogos
Gust G. Roupas
Samuel W. Rowe
John Rusnak
William P. Sanderson
Samuel Scarpino
Elmer Scheese
Donald C. Schieffer
Louise H. Schoenfeld
Michael Senkovich
Andrew Serenko
Michael J. Serina
John Shearer
William E. Sherman
Joseph Siebielec
Michael Sierdzinski
William Silagyi
John G. Simcik
Thomas Siple
Harry Skrocki
Stephen Skumsky
Louis Skurski
Charles Slavnik
William Smail
Joseph J. Snoha
Theodore F. Souchack
Edmund R. Sovia
Clifford T. Springer
George Sralik
Neal P. Stager
Frank E. Stancovich
Robert Stover
John M. Strauss
E. V. Stubblebine
Rudolph Supancic
Marlin Sweigert
Vernon Sybert
Joseph P. Szafransky
Joseph H. Taggart, Jr.
Charles J. Terry
Chester J. Trojan
John J. Trojan
Walter Tym
Rodney Walck

T. F. Weaver
Edward D. Weisenberg
Jean Weisenberg
Leon Weit
Joseph G. West
R. Westenberger
William Westenberger
Edward Wilkes
Carl Winkler
David Wolf
Wally Wolsky
Samuel J. Yeich
Henry Zale

Rhode Island
Rita Audette
Francis Boylan
John C. Brierce
Armand Durocher
Albert C. Geremia
Eleanor Hall
Lee H. Houle
Frank Martineau
Joseph Muratore
Aladino J. Ridolfi
Robert A. St. Jean

South Carolina
George Alexander
Wesley Farrell
David J. Hall
Jerry Hughes
J. G. Manor
Arthur Neighbors
Raymond P. Sullivan

Tennessee
John K. Rogers

Texas
Richard Anskimo
Everett Ballew
Jack Bird
Eddie Blackwell
Alvin Bradshaw
James W. Buster
J. R. Daniel
Franklin D. Evans
Pete Gunn
Orrin J. Henbest
B. J. Kilbrough
Charles W. Knapp
Thurman Lewis
Charles W. Nations
Donald H. Nehrkorn
Vernon Tunnell

Edward L. Wilson

Utah
Ethel E. Beasley
David K. Holther
Toby N. Larsen

Virginia
Herbert A. Fellers
Charles E. Grimm
Thomas E. Hurt, Jr.
Joseph H. Lieb

Washington
Elmer DePaul
Frank DeRosa
Alvin M. Keller
Adolph K. Mueller

West Virginia
Robert Ahalt
Thomas H. Armstrong

Wisconsin
Matthew Allen
Donald W. Baldini
Merle Barrington
Edward Barutha
Richard D. Baxter
Allen Behling
John Bontempo
Walter E. Bosnyak
George Bratel, Jr.
James Bucci
Wallace F. Buske
Nello J. Carloni
Willis Carvenough
Frank G. Casagrande
Richard E. Casagrande
Leo A. Checkai
Raymond E. Cherney
Lillian Cowling
Lucille J. Cowling
Al Dahlke
Enzo P. Decesari
Walter P. Dueno
Max Fenzl
A. J. Ferraro
Robert Freiburger
Gary J. Garofani
Louis J. Groppi
Mario A. Groppi
Rudolph Hackbarth
Donald Haznaw
Ralph Heller
William Higgins

Stanley Holewinski
George Hrabik, Jr.
J. M. Jagemann
Thaddeus Kantor
Harry Kaufman
Arthur W. Kehl
James Kofron
R. J. Kuchenreuther
Ernest G. Lucci
Harvey Mann
Fred J. Marchetti
Gilbert H. Mark
Leslie A. Markussen
Paul Marquardt
Kenneth Marth
Martin Martinetti
Edward F. Millane
John J. Millane
Arden Muchin
Joseph F. Naidl
Wilbert Ninmann
Joseph E. O'Herron
Alois Panfil
Mike Parish
Stephen Patti
Alfred Pauls
Joseph E. Perzentka
Ervin P. Peszka
Francis E. Pivonka
John E. Rastall
Robert E. Reichert
Nicholas V. Ricciardi
Richard Risch
Donald F. Ruffcorn
Arthur Schlei
Edward Schleis
Fred P. Schmidt
Robert S. Schmitz
Matthew Schwindt, Jr.
Theodore Sibinski
Eric L. Siffert
John P. Stanaitis
Joseph Tarala
Michael J. Terranova
Lewis W. Thompson
Alvin Titera
Joseph E. Travis
Edward Vieth, Jr.
Rupert S. Vono
Earl L. Witt
Americo J. Zanchetti

Posts & Departments

Alabama
Dept. Birmingham
0001 Montgomery
0023 Tuscaloosa
0025 Talladega
0036 Bessemer
0052 Decatur
0065 Kimberly
0088 Huntsville
0127 Birmingham
0216 Brookwood
0404 Tuscaloosa
0536 Birmingham
1001 Oxford
1159 Irondale
2912 Birmingham
3495 Birmingham
3517 Moody
7014 Birmingham

Alaska
Dept. Anchorage
0002 Anchorage
0004 Soldotna
0007 Fairbanks
0008 Seward
0009 Wasilla
0049 Anchorage

Arizona
Dept. Sierra Vista
0001 Melbourne
0002 Fort Smith
0010 Fayetteville
0027 Murfreesboro
0034 Hot Springs
0002 Apache Junction
0004 Kingman
0005 Phoenix
0011 Tucson
0012 Mesa
0013 Casa Grande
0015 Phoenix
0018 Prescott
0028 Phoenix
0039 Tucson
0044 Sierra Vista
0055 Douglas
0065 Phoenix
0089 Sierra Vista
0187 Apache Junction

California
Dept. Tulare ★
0001 Sacramento
0002 Culver City
0003 Santa Barbara
0004 Fresno
0006 San Jose
0008 Sacramento

0011 Garberville
0012 Modesto
0013 Jacumba
0014 Imperial
0015 Poplar
0017 El Cajon
0018 Anaheim
0019 Stockton
0020 Adelanto
0021 San Fernando
0022 Visalia,
0025 San Francisco
0026 Brentwood
0027 Sun City
0028 Salinas
0029 Yreka
0030 Gardena
0032 Ventura
0033 Wilmington
0034 San Francisco
0048 Long Beach
0049 Hanford
0050 Poplar
0053 San Mateo
0055 Goleta
0056 Tulare
0057 Woodville
0062 La Puente
0065 Tulare
0070 Corona
0072 Fresno
0077 Porterville
0080 Anaheim
0088 Alhambra
0098 Sanger
0100 Chino
0101 Yountville
0107 Redlands
0111 Buena Park
0113 Irwindale
0117 Costa Mesa
0165 Sacramento
0177 Van Nuys
0256 Morro Bay
0589 Fawnskin
0777 Santa Cruz
0888 Los Angeles
0901 Sacramento
1944 Los Angeles
1946 San Diego
1969 Tulare
1977 Lake Elsinore
1988 Porterville
1989 Livermore
1990 Stockton
4942 National City
5277 Barstow
7093 Temeucla
8088 Los Angeles
9442 Spring Valley

9936 Portola

Canada
0001 Espanola

China (Taiwan)
0002 Taipei
0009 Tai-Chung

Colorado
0001 Denver
0003 Elizabeth
0010 Grand Junction

Connecticut
Dept. Norwich ★
0001 West Haven
0002 Windham
0009 North Haven
0012 Norwich
0018 Enfield
0043 Ansonia
0045 Danielson
0047 Moosup
0050 Willimantic
0083 Meriden/Wallingford

District of Columbia
Dept.
0007
0109
0015
0022
0008

Florida
Dept. North Miami ★
0001 St. Petersburg
0002 Tamarac
0003 Ft. Lauderdale
0004 Tampa
0005 St Petersburg
0006 Vero Beach
0008 St Petersburg
0009 Odessa
0011 North Miami Beach
0012 Pensacola
0014 Hobe Sound
0015 Ft. Pierce
0016 Hudson
0017 Sanford
0018 Winter Park
0020 St. Augustine
0027 Cocoa
0029 Mary Easter
0030 Orlando
0032 Lakeland
0035 Crestview
0036 Key West
0040 Naranja

0046 Orlando
0047 Panama City Beach
0050 N. Ft. Myers
0060 Arcadia
0077 Merritt Island
0078 Valparaiso
0081 N. Ft. Myers
0085 Bonifay
0086 Keystone Heights
0092 Port St. Lucie
0093 Interlachen
0094 Fedhaven
0099 Ocala
0100 Daytona Beach
0151 Jacksonville
0178 DeFuniak Springs
0231 Fountain
0292 Pensacola
0500 Daytona Beach
0549 Panama City
0793 Lake Panasoffkee
0893 Rockledge
0935 Islamorada
1292 Milton
1987 Titusville
1992 Eustis
2298 Callaway
2473 Clearwater
7467 Pinellas Park

Georgia
Dept. Atlanta ★
0001 Atlanta
0002 Macon
0005 Augusta
0009 Muscogee
0010 Athens
0017 Forest Park
0018 Atlanta
0022 Toccoa
0033 Washington
0048 LaFayette
0055 Bremen
0062 Dublin
0066 Young Harris
0092 Trion
0097 Newnan
0108 Rome
0110 Tennille
0600 Toccoa
0607 Valdosta
0617 Atlanta
0621 Waycross

Germany
0004 Babehnausen

Hawaii
0001 Johnston Island

★ Continuous operation since Dec. 31, 1947

Idaho
0027 Twin Falls

Illinois
Dept. Springfield ★
0001 Chicago
0002 Chicago
0003 Champaign
0004 Mt. Vernon
0005 Chicago
0006 Carbondale
0007 Chicago
0008 Knoxville
0009 Skokie
0011 Macomb
0013 Chicago
0014 Clinton
0015 Mt. Carmel
0016 Litchfield
0017 Chicago
0018 Chicago
0019 Hoopeston
0020 Gillespie
0021 Carthage
0022 Villa Grove
0023 Rushville
0024 Berwyn
0025 Carpentersville
0026 Olney
0027 Salem
0029 Taylorville
0030 Ottawa
0032 Freeport
0033 Robinson
0034 Chicago
0035 Waukegan
0036 Chicago
0039 Rockford
0040 Effingham
0041 Marshall
0042 Chicago
0043 Burnham
0044 Pana
0047 Chicago
0049 Decatur
0050 Aurora
0051 Granite City
0052 Fisher
0053 Morris
0055 Mt. Olive
0057 Carterville
0060 Grand Tower
0061 Springfield
0064 Peoria
0066 Wheeling
0067 Beecher
0070 Vandalia
0071 Lincoln
0072 Worth
0076 Ursa

0077 Chillicothe
0078 LaSalle
0080 Chicago
0083 Bethalto
0084 Crete
0086 LaHarpe
0089 Lombard
0090 DeKalb
0091 Hampshire
0092 Rantoul
0094 Springfield
0097 Berwyn
0099 Brookfield
0100 Jacksonville
0103 Aurora
0104 Quincy
0107 Manteno
0108 Carlinville
0109 Chicago
0111 Chicago
0113 Bradley
0114 Godfrey
0116 Pontiac
0120 Streator
0121 Greenup
0123 Dixon
0128 Shelbyville
0132 Metropolis
0133 Paris
0136 Havana
0140 Greenville
0145 East Moline
0148 Waltonville
0149 West Frankfort
0152 Chicago
0156 Waterloo
0161 Scott AFB
0164 Monmouth
0167 Sterling
0169 North Pekin
0179 Greenview
0192 Chicago
0202 Elgin
0204 Madison
0235 Pekin
0243 Chicago
0245 Cary
0247 Chicago
0250 Round Lake
0252 Chicago
0255 Buffalo Grove
0256 Springfield
0257 Springfield
0267 Jerseyville
0268 Glenwood
0269 Woodstock
0270 Normal
0274 Bloomington
0276 Elliott
0277 Streamwood

0278 Colfax

Indiana
Dept. Connersville ★
0001 Plymouth
0002 Terre Haute
0003 Osgood
0004 Jeffersonville
0005 Marion
0006 Gary
0007 North Vernon
0009 Evansdale
0011 Connersville
0012 Muncie
0013 Brookville
0015 Cedar Lake
0016 Wabash
0017 Dillsboro
0020 Michigan City
0023 Hartford City
0025 Markleville
0026 Pendleton
0033 Fort Wayne
0038 Greensfork
0043 Warsaw
0045 Hammond
0046 Angola
0056 Aurora
0061 Rockville
0064 Whiting
0066 South Bend
0077 Sullivan
0079 West Lafayette
0084 Evansville
0091 Monticello
0099 Indianapolis
0100 Indianapolis
0123 Indianapolis
0146 Michigan City
0692 Anderson

Iowa
Dept. Des Moines ★
0001 Atlantic
0002 Des Moines
0003 Dubuque
0004 Fort Dodge
0006 Cedar Rapids
0008 Shenandoah
0009 Carlisle
0010 Lincoln
0013 Peosta
0015 Guttenberg
0016 Lowden
0017 Grundy Center
0019 Waterloo
0025 Marshalltown
0027 Monona
0028 Clinton
0030 Clarksville

0031 Evansdale
0037 Central City
0039 Havelock
0041 Rockwell City
0042 Pomeroy
0045 Walnut
0049 Cedar Falls
0051 Kimballton
0062 Andrew
0064 Baldwin
0066 Storm Lake
0077 Algona
0079 Waverly
0080 Gladbrook
0082 Hudson
0083 Kesley
0088 Allison
0090 Fredericksburg
0091 Wellsburg
0092 Mason City
0095 Palmer
0100 Marshalltown
0102 Aplington
0106 Bristow
0107 Richmond
0108 McGregor
0109 Shell Rock
0110 Anamosa
0129 Ireton
0135 Clear Lake
0136 Des Moines
0138 Centerville
0140 Preston
0143 Indianola
0144 Davenport
0150 Charlotte
0151 Bettendorf
0152 Council Bluffs

Kansas
Dept. Hutchinson
0001 Olathe
0011 Hutchinson
0031 Pittsburg
0033 McPherson
0036 Wichita
0042 Neodesha
0069 Kansas City
0071 Eldorado
0089 Salina
1890 Ft. Dodge
1984 Manhattan

Kentucky
Dept. Louisville ★
0001 Louisville
0002 Louisville
0009 Louisville
0027 Martin
0056 Paducah

Posts & Departments

0058 Silver Grove
0061 Louisville
0064 Lewisburg
0074 Catlettsburg
0075 Owensboro
0076 Madisonville
0078 Oak Grove
0085 Covington
0087 Catlettsburg
0095 Greenup
0099 Warfield
0100 Danville
0101 Corbin
0102 LaGrange
0103 Vine Grove
0104 Harlan
0105 Mt. Washington
0106 Henderson

Korea
0001 Seoul

Louisiana
Dept. New Orleans ★
0002 Baton Rouge
0005 Monroe
0007 Alexandria
0008 Albany
0038 Westwego
0041 Arabi
0047 Chalmette
0049 River Ridge
0063 Harvey
0065 Belle Chasse
0066 Monroe
0067 Jackson
0068 Springfield
0100 Abita Springs
1990 West Monroe

Maine
Dept. Portland ★
0001 Biddeford
0002 Yarmouth
0003 Sanford
0004 Franklin
0005 Old Orchard Beach
0006 New Gloucester
0010 Freeport
0012 Woolwich
0013 Durham
0014 Augusta
0015 Westbrook
0017 Houlton
0020 Arundel
0025 Portland
0033 Jay
1946 Lyman
1976 South Portland
1993 Enfield

Maryland
Dept. Hagerstown
0001 Prince Georges Cty
0002 Frederick
0003 Ft. Meade
0004 Salisbury
0005 Frederick
0007 Thurmont
0008 Baltimore
0009 Middletown
0010 Hagerstown
0011 Cresaptown
0012 Rockville
0013 La Plata
0014 Cascade
0033 Baltimore
0100 Jefferson
0115 Riverdale

Massachusetts
Dept. Boston ★
0001 Roslindale
0002 Cambridge
0003 Boston
0004 Somerville
0007 Quincy
0012 Chicopee
0013 Boston
0014 Watertown
0015 Chelsea
0017 Plymouth
0018 Northbridge
0021 Melrose
0027 Lynn
0028 Dorchester
0029 Fitchburg
0032 Gloucester
0037 Westfield
0038 Leominster
0041 Watertown
0048 Winthrop
0051 Randolph
0053 Salem
0060 Fall River
0061 Taunton
0062 New Bedford
0065 North Attleboro
0070 Falmouth
0072 Somerset
0074 Three Rivers
0079 Natick
0125 Everett
0128 Dorchester
0129 Southbridge
0145 Wakefield
0146 Dorchester
0147 Haverhill
0161 Lynn
0201 Ipswich
0208 Hudson

0209 Bedford
0211 Dorchester
0391 Charlton
0495 Millis
0640 Tewksbury
0793 Athol
1391 Worcester
1972 Norton
1977 Stoughton
1980 Marlboro
1984 Mattapan
1991 Chatham

Michigan
Dept. Detroit ★
0004 Dearborn
0006 Detroit
0007 Chesterfield
0008 Detroit
0009 Detroit
0013 Higgins Lake
0014 Hamtramck
0021 Detroit
0022 Bay City
0023 Kentwood
0027 Detroit
0028 Jackson
0029 Mount Clemens
0030 Comstock Park
0032 Lansing
0033 Detroit
0035 Wyoming
0040 Trout Lake
0045 Detroit
0049 Detroit
0052 New Baltimore
0053 Livonia
0054 Detroit
0055 Detroit
0056 Detroit
0057 Harper Woods
0060 Detroit
0066 Battle Creek
0069 Detroit
0072 New Haven
0074 Kalamazoo
0076 Novi
0077 Dearborn
0079 Goetzville
0080 Saginaw
0082 Ludington
0088 St. Joseph
0090 Grayling
0093 Armada
0098 Grand Rapids
0099 Wyandotte
0104 Standish
0110 Cadillac
0114 Elk Rapids
0115 Port Hope

0120 Mesick
0121 St. Clair Shores
0122 Ishpeming
0123 Escanaba
0126 Grand Rapids
0131 Dearborn Heights
0144 Rose City
0171 Westland
0259 Bronson
0347 Ypsilanti
0419 Pinckney
0436 Iron River
0490 Ironwood
0588 Edmore
0777 Iron Mountain
0910 Detroit
1001 Flint
1072 Kingston
1234 Kent City
1776 Coldwater
1812 Rockwood
1824 Tecumseh
1899 Kinross
1941 Big Rapids
1957 Adrian
1978 Niles
1983 Holland
1988 Baldwin
1991 Sault Ste Marie
1993 Fennville
2000 Whitehall
3720 Swartz Creek
5114 Camden

Minnesota
Dept. Waseca
0001 Mendota
0002 Rochester
0003 Ponemah
0005 Fergus Falls
0006 Minneapolis
0007 Faribault
0008 Aitkin
0010 Minneapolis
0012 Hibbing
0013 Waconia
0015 Hopkins
0017 Cloquet
0018 Merrifield
0019 Lake City
0020 Albany
0021 Detroit Lakes
0023 Owatonna
0024 St. Paul
0026 Ironton
0027 Effie
0028 Carlton
0031 Waseca
0034 Ortonville
0036 Alexandria

★ Continuous operation since Dec. 31, 1947

0040 Cass Lake
0050 Aurora
0053 Onamia
0175 Olivia
0251 Robbinsdale
0290 Morris
0601 Champlin

Mississippi
Dept. Jackson
0001 Jackson
0017 Brandon
0019 Cleveland
0020 Vicksburg
0350 Iuka
0355 Tupelo
1986 Picayune
1988 Horn Lake
1989 Grenada

Missouri
Dept. St. Louis ★
0001 Kirkwood
0002 St. Louis
0006 St. Louis
0011 St. Louis
0013 St. Louis
0029 Poplar Bluff
0041 St. Louis
0042 Herculaneum
0048 DeSoto
0055 Berkeley
0056 Ballwin
0063 Kansas City
0067 St. Louis
0069 Kirkwood
0088 St. Louis
0091 St. Louis
0094 Perryville
0095 Kansas City
0098 West Plains
0106 St. Peters
0108 Rocky Mount
0111 Kansas City
0113 Farmington
0114 Flemington
0116 Stockton
0117 Buffalo
0120 Urich
0121 Norwood
0123 Squires
0124 Davisville
0125 Van Buren
0127 Mountain View
0128 Doniphan
0130 Kennett
0131 Nevada
0135 Thayer
0137 St. Louis
0138 Kennett

0140 Cardwell
0141 Poplar Bluff
0142 Jefferson City
0143 Knob Noster
0145 Arnold
0146 Ava
0147 Hermitage
0148 Steele
0149 Sikeston
0150 Osceola
0151 New Franklin
0152 Lexington
0153 Steedman
0154 Isbella
0155 Auxuasse
0156 St. Louis
0157 Marshall Junction
0158 Mountain Grove
0178 Brighton

Montana
0001 Kalispell
0003 Missoula
0090 Billings

Nebraska
0001 South Sioux City

The Netherlands
0001 Nuland

Nevada
0001 Searchlight

New Hampshire
0001 Nashua
0002 Salem
0003 Manchester
0711 Claremont

New Jersey
Dept. Lyndhurst ★
0002 Jackson
0005 Newark
0011 Glendora
0012 Irvington
0013 Garfield
0016 Bridgewater
0020 Lyndhurst
0022 West New York
0025 Elizabeth
0026 Belleville
0030 Nutley
0032 Bayonne
0033 Jersey City
0034 Brunswick
0035 Jersey City
0070 East Orange
0077 Gloucester
0079 Mt. Holly

0089 Pine Beach
0101 Delair
0251 Delran
0711 Northfield
1776 Trenton

New Mexico
Dept. Albuquerque
0005 Las Cruces
0007 Albuquerque
0011 Madrid
0012 Two Grey Hills
0013 Alamagordo
0014 Clovis
0021 Belen
0028 Los Lunas

New York
Dept. Blasdell ★
0001 Cuba
0002 Palmyra
0004 Massena
0005 Buffalo
0008 Malone
0013 Buffalo
0014 Depew
0017 Buffalo
0018 East Islip
0019 Ogdensburg
0021 Amsterdam
0026 North Tonawanda
0027 Brooklyn
0028 Richmond Hill
0032 Amsterdam
0034 Ridgewood
0035 Schenectady
0038 Bronx
0040 Yonkers
0044 Hicksville
0045 Buffalo
0049 Amherst
0050 Albany
0066 Buffalo
0072 Buffalo
0076 Bay Shore
0077 Glen Falls
0088 Massapequa
0100 Long Beach
0101 Brooklyn
0111 Patchogue
0116 Staten Island
0219 Concord
0324 Buffalo
0333 Endicott
0777 Ilion
1097 Rochester
1420 Buffalo
1473 Randolph
1829 Rochester
1887 Angola

1946 Tonawanda
1986 Melville
3076 Buffalo
8113 West Seneca

North Carolina
Dept. Lexington ★
0005 Asheville
0013 Shelby
0042 Shelby
0043 Roxboro
0240 Denton
0320 Roanoke Rapids
0460 Salisbury
0565 Salisbury
0635 Raleigh
0665 Fairview
0730 Henderson
0760 Welcome
0777 Winston-Salem
0820 Mooresville
0835 Lexington
0845 Rockwell
0905 Asheboro
0910 Albemarle
0920 Gastonia
0935 Winston-Salem
0955 Lincolnton
0970 Fayetteville
0980 Connelly Springs
0985 Eden
0990 High Point
0995 Kings Mountain
0999 Salisbury

North Dakota
Dept. Fargo
0003 Valley City
0004 Jamestown
0005 Enderlin
0007 Fargo
0008 West Fargo
0009 Bismarck
0010 Minot
0011 Grafton
0015 Beulah
0016 Wahpeton
0017 Harvey
0018 Fort Totten
0019 Grand Forks

Ohio
Dept. Columbus ★
0001 Lima
0002 Hamilton
0003 Delaware
0004 Chillicothe
0005 Cleveland
0006 Massillon
0007 Cuyahoga Falls

Posts & Departments

0009 Dayton	0083 Cleveland	1963 Cincinnati	1874 Baker City
0011 Solon	0084 Jackson	1965 Norwalk	1984 Salem
0012 Massillon	0086 Cincinnati	1967 Gnaden Hutten	1993 McMinnville
0013 Shelby	0087 Mt. Gilead	1968 Montville	
0014 Xenia	0088 Troy	1969 Hayesville	**Pennsylvania**
0015 Bedford	0089 Columbus	1971 Perry	Dept. Pottsville ★
0017 Sandusky	0091 St. Marys	1974 Columbus	0002 York
0019 London	0092 Antwerp	1977 Warren	0003 Reading
0020 Kenton	0093 Albany	1979 Galion	0007 Shenandoah
0021 Findlay	0095 Mount Vernon	1983 Hamilton	0008 McKeesport
0022 Vermilion	0096 Ashland	1985 Lancaster	0010 Harrisburg
0023 Gallipolis	0099 Vandalia	1986 Sidney	0017 Easton
0024 Dayton	0100 Swanton	1988 Cincinnati	0019 Lancaster
0025 Springfield	0101 Niles	1989 Cleveland	0022 Hanover
0026 Mansfield	0102 Delaware	1990 Medina	0028 Pittsburgh
0027 Bucyrus	0104 Delaware	1991 Defiance	0034 Pittsburgh
0028 Marysville	0105 Bellafontaine	1992 Zanesville	0040 New Holland
0030 Galion	0106 Niles	1993 Rickenbacker Airport	0044 Gordon
0031 Mansfield	0109 Mentor-on-the-Lake	2001 Columbus	0055 Oakmont
0032 Elyria	0111 Woodlawn	2256 Circleville	0059 Wilkes-Barre
0033 Dayton	0112 Newton Falls	3623 Greensburg	0060 Braddock
0034 Youngstown	0120 Franklin	4077 Dennison	0064 Pittsburgh
0035 Youngstown	0121 Urbana		0066 Edwardsville
0036 Coshocton	0123 Dover	**Oklahoma**	0072 Minersville
0037 Enon	0124 Canton	Dept. Oklahoma City	0073 Pittsburgh
0038 Bloomingdale	0125 Beach City	0001 Welch	0077 Philadelphia
0039 Lakeview	0131 Milford	0003 Valliant	0080 Shamokin
0040 Mentor	0141 Willow Wood	0004 Ratliff City	0083 Lansford
0041 Cincinnati	0146 Washington C.H.	0005 Tulsa	0085 Export
0042 Marion	0148 Medway	0006 Adair	0088 Greensburg
0043 Bellville	0149 Polk	0007 Antlers	0090 Johnstown
0044 Youngstown	0162 Huntington	0008 Grove	0094 United
0045 Salem	0176 Richfield	0009 Norman	0100 Philadelphia
0046 Huber Heights	0189 Springfield	0010 Lawton	0101 Tamaqua
0047 Lorain	0212 Norwood	0011 Duncan	0103 Hopwood
0048 Tiffin	0222 Akron	0012 Edmond	0106 Lehighton
0049 Huron	0250 Wooster	0013 Oklahoma City	0114 Summit Station
0051 Thornville	0290 Vienna Township	0014 McAlester	0116 Shenandoah
0052 Toledo	0300 Columbus	0015 Poteau	0118 Morton
0053 Chauncey	0342 New Lexington	0016 Shawnee	0122 Thompsontown
0054 Bryan	0345 Newark	0017 Hobart	0132 Bradenville
0055 Sheffield Lake	0357 Dayton	0018 Granite	0136 Ephrata
0056 Portsmouth	0377 Springfield	0020 Enid	0142 St. Clair
0057 Leipsic	0444 Fairborn	0027 Lawton	0146 Philadelphia
0058 Piketon	0492 Hicksville	0031 Taft	0148 Philadelphia
0059 Centerburg	0555 Canton	0099 Midwest City	0150 Portage
0060 Cleveland	0620 Marion		0153 Columbia
0061 Hillsboro	0692 Holland	**Oregon**	0156 Lavelle
0064 McArthur	0711 Bowling Green	Dept. Portland	0158 Philadelphia
0065 Brecksville	0726 Eldorado	0001 Portland	0159 Philipsburg
0066 Covington	0777 Upper Sandusky	0005 Roseburg	0172 Fairfield
0069 Fostoria	0969 Columbus	0006 Portland	0180 Pottsville
0070 Cambridge	1010 Toledo	0008 Coos Bay	0189 Pittston
0071 Fairfield	1312 Columbus	0009 Oregon City	0198 Philadelphia
0072 Piqua	1313 Napoleon	0010 Coos Bay	0209 Schuylkill Haven
0073 Cleveland	1338 New Philadelphia	0012 Bandon	0211 LLewellyn
0075 Coshocton	1714 Lordstown	0013 Sweet Home	0224 Chambersburg
0076 Athens	1776 Logan	0015 Albany	0252 Philadelphia
0077 Ashtabula	1788 Marietta	0016 Springfield	0253 White Haven
0080 Maple Heights	1928 Columbus	1776 Independence	0256 New Philadelphia

★ Continuous operation since Dec. 31, 1947

0261 Towanda
0268 North Huntington
0270 Olyphant
0272 Butler
0273 Southampton
0274 Carlisle
0276 Middletown
0277 Indiana
0278 West Newton
0280 Erie
0281 New Castle
0282 Arnold
0283 Gilbert
0284 Nazareth
0285 Sayre
0286 Harrisburg
0287 Easton
0288 Allentown

Rhode Island
Dept. Providence ★
0001 Forestdale
0003 Providence
0004 Coventry
0006 West Warwick
0007 Woonsocket
0008 Central Falls
0009 North Providence
0011 Cumberland
0012 Woonsocket
0013 Providence
0015 Warwick
0022 Cranston
0033 Pawtucket
0037 Bristol

South Carolina
Dept. Columbia
0002 Columbia
0021 Columbia
0024 North Charleston
0031 Charleston Heights
0034 Orangeburg
0042 Surfside Beach
0058 Spartanburg
0070 Port Royal
0073 Columbia
0074 Columbia
0075 Greenville
0078 Camden
0080 Sumter
0501 Myrtle Beach

South Dakota
0001 Belle Fourche

Tennessee
Dept. Chattanooga
0002 Oak Ridge
0007 Morristown

0013 Cleveland
0014 Clarksville
0023 Nashville
0029 College Grove
0031 Watauga
0032 Lenoir City
0037 Kingsport
0040 Cookeville
0045 Buchanan
0047 Crossville
0050 Johnson City
0052 Dickson
0056 Sparta
0057 Shiloh
0070 Harriman
0075 Newport
0077 Gray
0086 Memphis
0090 Decatur
0100 Etowah
0101 Smithville

Texas
Dept. Beaumont
0001 Brownwood
0002 Houston
0003 Diboll
0004 Dalla
0005 Houston
0006 Houston
0008 Dallas
0010 Mesquite
0012 Grape Creek
0013 Rye
0014 Midland
0016 Abilene
0017 Dallas
0019 Axtell
0020 Brownwood
0021 Dallas
0022 Dallas
0023 Rockwall
0024 East Tawakoni
0026 San Angelo
0028 Terrell
0029 Amarillo
0031 Rowlett
0032 Comanche
0035 Waco
0036 Quinlan
0037 San Antonio
0038 Terrell
0039 Irving
0041 Waco
0042 Balch Springs
0043 Comanche
0044 Ennis
0047 Sherman
0052 Dallas
0053 Arlington

0056 Mart
0057 Greenville
0058 Harker Heights
0063 Larado
0065 Marfa
0066 Irving
0068 Tyler
0069 Garland
0071 Richardson
0072 Hillsboro
0073 Dallas
0074 Houston
0076 Ft. Worth
0077 Red Oak
0078 Tyler
0079 Dallas
0080 Lampasas
0081 Galveston
0083 Decatur
0087 Mesquite
0089 Grand Prairie
0090 Houston
0091 Ballinger
0092 Gun Barrel
0095 Ft. Worth
0096 Greenville
0097 Brownwood
0099 Dallas

Utah
0001 Ogden

Virginia
Dept. Dumfries
0001 Richmond
0002 Woodbridge
0003 Fredericksburg
0005 Bristol
0012 Jonesville
0013 Colonial Beach
0030 Hampton
0035 Collinsville
0040 Roanoke
0069 Norfolk
0082 Alexandria
0089 Salem

Washington
Dept. Tacoma
0001 Tacoma
0002 Olympia
0003 Seattle
0005 Tacoma
0006 Port Townsend
0020 Randle
0028 Pasco

West Virginia
Dept. Mt. Gay
0034 Parkersburg

0035 Huntington
0038 Falling Waters
0050 Dunbar
0060 South Charleston
0077 Nitro
0090 Huntington
0119 Danville
0169 Milton
0316 Point Pleasant
0631 Nitro
0777 Mt. Gay
1619 Charleston
1990 Huntington

Wisconsin
Dept. Milwaukee ★
0003 South Milwaukee
0004 South Milwaukee
0005 Menomonee
0006 Marinette
0007 Oshkosh
0010 Shawano
0011 Green Bay
0013 Redgranite
0014 Milwaukee
0018 Sheboygan
0023 Manitowoc
0025 Dallas
0027 Milwaukee
0030 Appleton
0035 Watertown
0037 Milwaukee
0042 Kewaunee Co.
0045 New London
0051 Sturgeon Bay
0059 Milwaukee
0060 Milwaukee
0061 Milwaukee
0063 Oconto
0071 West Allis
0072 Connorsville
0099 Manitowoc
0120 Racine
0128 Rice Lake
0160 Pulaski
0190 Spooner
1032 Reedsville
1051 Stevens Point
1887 King
1947 Two Rivers
1993 Hertel
5494 Black River Falls
5700 Greenfield

Wyoming
1065 Cheyenne
1990 Cheyenne

List compiled 4/15/94

Index

Italicized page number indicates photograph

Index

Italicized page number indicates photograph

Index

Index

Italicized page number indicates photograph

Index

Index

Italicized page number indicates photograph

1993–94 National Executive Committee

Alabama
Charles Casmus, Jr., NEC
W. Tom Parkes, Alt. NEC

Alaska
Roger Smith, NEC
Paul Plaas, Alt. NEC

Arizona
Fred A. Jervis, NEC
Barney Interest, Alt. NEC

California
Manuel Brazil, Jr., NEC
Manuel Toledo, Alt. NEC

Connecticut
Michael Grip, Jr., NEC
Woodrow W. White, Alt. NEC

District of Columbia
Johnnie Collins, Jr., NEC
Ira A. Jett, Alt. NEC

Florida
Ralph E. Hall, NEC
Carl E. Jasinski, Alt. NEC

Georgia
William Bates, NEC
Henry Lee Chiles, Alt. NEC

Illinois
Donald Russell, NEC
S. John Sisler, Alt. NEC

Indiana
George E. Brattain, Sr., NEC
Edward Baker, Alt. NEC

Iowa
Orvin Schoville, NEC
Robert E. Schoon, Alt. NEC

Kansas
Ronald Anderson, Sr., NEC
Robert Pitts, Alt. NEC

Kentucky
John Melcher, NEC
William Eversole, Alt. NEC

Louisiana
Evans St. Romain, NEC
Herbert Hayes, Alt. NEC

Maine
Gene Kiely, NEC
Ray Cloutier, Alt. NEC

Maryland
Theodore Byran, NEC
Robert W. Kight, Alt. NEC

Massachusetts
Guy Massa, NEC
James M. Willey, Alt. NEC

Michigan
Frank Krzesowik, NEC
Jasper T. McCain, Alt. NEC

Minnesota
Michael Nelson, NEC
Gene Richgels, Alt. NEC

Mississippi
Robert Neely, Sr., NEC
Brent Simpson, Alt. NEC

Missouri
John Huff, NEC
Chester Spangler, Alt. NEC

New Jersey
Donald E. Feldman, NEC
Nelson W. Rummel, Alt. NEC

New Mexico
Lyndon Vibbard, NEC
Dale Howard, Alt. NEC

New York
Leon Gubala, NEC
Richard May, Alt. NEC

North Carolina
Carl E. Ritchie, NEC
Jimmy L. Ely, Alt. NEC

North Dakota
Kenneth M. Evenson, NEC
John E. Adolf, Alt. NEC

Ohio
Austin Wilson, NEC
Fred W. Large, Alt. NEC

Oklahoma
Lee Moore, NEC
Jerry Stewart, Alt. NEC

Oregon
Charles Altig, Sr., NEC
Carl Swinyer, Alt. NEC

Pennsylvania
John Soltis, NEC
Arthur C. Stahl, Alt. NEC

Rhode Island
Roger Fortier, NEC
Joseph G.A. Riccio, Alt. NEC

South Carolina
Robert F. Lewis, Sr., NEC
Harold F. Slawson, Alt. NEC

Tennessee
William G. Kilgore, NEC
John T. Eskew, Alt. NEC

Texas
Bobby W. Webb, NEC
Richard Jaworski, Alt. NEC

Virginia
David L. Rose, NEC
Enid Anderson, Alt. NEC

Washington
Anthony Petrarca, NEC
Michael Henson, Alt. NEC

West Virginia
Thomas Teasley, NEC
Albert Kinney, Alt. NEC

Wisconsin
Edward DeNomie, NEC
William Stys, Alt. NEC